THE RITUAL QUEEN

UNCENSORED

A guide to putting on your big girl panties

First edition

ISBN: 9798514112135

This book was professionally typeset on Reedsy.
Find out more at reedsy.com

For Earl. Who always brings me out of the darkness and back into love.

To find yourself,
you have to love yourself.

To love yourself,
you have to know your worth.

To know your worth,
you have to find validation within.

To find validation within,
you have to stop listening to outside sources.

THERESA TIRK

Contents

Foreword		ii
Introduction		vi
1	The Breaking Point	1
2	Childhood	14
3	Monkey See, Monkey Do	26
4	Growing Up and Getting Out	35
5	Knocked Up	44
6	Nuptials	55
7	Cutting Ties	61
8	Martyrdom	69
9	Tick Tick Boom	79
10	Turning Points	87
11	Coming Full Circle	101
Resources - Essential Oil Blends		109
Resources - Forgiveness Work		111
Resources - Meet Gail		113
Resources - Affirmations		115
Angel Numbers Guidebook		117
REVIVE AND THRIVE Ritual		124
Acknowledgements		130
About the Author		132
Also by The Ritual Queen		133

Foreword

Hiding the truth of who we are always seems easier until it becomes wildly uncomfortable. It is that feeling of being so deeply inauthentic and disconnected from who we are that we have no choice but to stop ourselves dead in our tracks and ask, "Who the hell am I?"

This was a huge part of my personal development journey. Over committing myself to things and people that didn't serve me and hiding behind the allure of pleasing others desperately hoping for acceptance.

It took me four years of selling real estate with my boyfriend in his family business for me to be honest with myself and realize I was only selling homes to gain that elusive feeling of being accepted every time I would proudly call my now mother-in-law to tell her I put a house under contract.

It was in those moments I felt that false high state of external validation, and inside, I was begging my higher power to guide me to my true purpose and inner freedom.

It wasn't until I got real with myself and hit some major breaking points that I discovered the path to my purpose was here the whole time. All of the discomfort and lack of connection was part of the greater plan.

Becoming a life coach and now a coach that trains other coaches, I hear the huge cries of humanity desperately wanting to stop hiding and step out into their light.

Everything I went through on my journey is what led me to help others.

Everything you are going through is what is leading you to your truth, including this book.

One of the first programs I ever created was a course called, "Create Your Life On Purpose." It was a program to help find you're calling and connect to your purpose.

Theresa Tirk purchased that program and upgraded to a one on one coaching call. The moment we got on that call and started coaching, I knew this woman was going to make a massive impact on the world.

Her story brought me to tears and the way she was able to share it with me was powerful.

When our call was coming to an end…. I looked at Theresa and said, I feel like our work together is just getting started, she agreed.

Watching Theresa transform before my eyes and fully embody her calling all the while moving through deep depression, anxiety and panic attacks. She is a perfect model to empower us all to step into our authentic self, while not denying our emotions.

I watched her show up on social media, even when she wasn't feeling her best.

I watched her inspire her community, teaching and leading by being vulnerable and real.

That is true success in my eyes.

Being an inspiration is no longer measured by perfection.

Success is no longer a product of "having it all together all the time."

I have watched Theresa step into her truth, purpose and uncensored self by honoring who she is, what she desires and following her intuition and passion.

Now she is a published author, coach and inspiration to so many showing us all that no matter how you were born into the world, what hand you were dealt, how much addiction and trauma you have endured, you have the power to heal and show others what is possible.

This book will radically shift your life if you let it. You have to first be willing to put on your big girl panties, as she will remind you.

Theresa has a story to share that will touch your heart and hold up a bold mirror of truth. Are you willing to see yourself?

I couldn't be more proud of my dear friend and client. Theresa Tirk is a force to be reckoned with. You will thank her from the depths of your soul for her courageous journey and it will give you the hope and loving kick in the booty you need to wake up to your truth, breakthrough your past and live a life of joy.

In the "Create Your Life On Purpose" program Theresa shared her calling statement, "I help women be their own validation so they can radiate love."

Yes, yes you do, Theresa. Thank you for your work in the world.

Get ready for all the sass and class and know that with every page you turn you are shifting into the best version of yourself. I am sending you so much love on your journey.

Ashley Gordon

Introduction

Hello. My name is Theresa and I am a recovering people-pleaser. I am also a wife, a mom, and so many other things too! With all of these titles comes more expectations, opinions, and you guessed it, more people pleasing! I decided to write this book and share my stories with the hopes it will bring you some comfort, inspiration, healing, and laughter. A book that is based on my perception and opinions of my life.

I'm not gonna lie, this is also a selfish project as part of my healing journey. You see, I've been on a journey of healing, self-discovery, and development for a few years now. In my early 40's when I was finally able to muster up enough courage to admit I needed help and ask for it, I was diagnosed with severe depression, anxiety, and panic attacks. That was the start of what will be a lifelong journey of inner work. It never really ends, which came as a shock to me. Seriously. I figured once I did all the therapy, twisted myself into a pretzel with all those crazy-ass yoga moves, sat cross-legged on a meditation pillow for hours on end, and unleashed the demons within onto paper, I'd be healed. A sparkly white light would shine down onto my golden locks and I'd be one with the Universe and at peace within.

Newsflash lady, that elusive unicorn is still fucking hiding from me. I have now come to terms with the fact that as much as I can look back over the last few years and realize just how far I have actually come, I can also look forward and know that the work will forever be happening and I'm okay with that. Crazy as it is, I actually like doing all this stuff. I know, you are probably rolling your eyes at me thinking, "yeah ok bitch, inner work is fun, sure thing." Slow your roll girl, I didn't say fun, I said I like it, but yes there are times where healing and working on yourself can actually be fun.

This journey I've been on has allowed me to meet some amazing women and to explore options that I had no clue existed. I've become a certified aromatherapist, a certified life coach, level 1 Reiki certified, a published author (fingers crossed), and I know that there is so much more on the horizon.

Four years ago, I would have never dreamed any of that would exist in my world. I had trouble getting out of bed and brushing my teeth on a daily basis, normal everyday functions were a huge challenge. The thought of a career that I loved helping others, was not even a blimp on my radar. In all honesty, yes, a journey of self-discovery is hard, it gets ugly, you want to say fuck it and quit more times that you can count, but it's also beautiful, freeing, and healing. And we are so worth all the effort.

If you are on your journey, keep going! Even on the days where it's hard as shit and you want to walk away, keep going. If you haven't started your journey yet and the thoughts of it feel overwhelming, just start. One foot in front of the other, one baby step at a time. You got this. You see, we can do hard things. Sometimes life is hard. It can be hard to live in fear, overwhelm, and darkness. It can be hard to face those fears, to try and find a way out of the darkness, to fight back against the overwhelm. The difference is one path never changes, it will always be overwhelming, cloaked in darkness, fear, and sadness. The second path might be scary, it might be dark, it might be so overwhelming it takes your breath away, but at the end of that path is sunshine, joy, hope, and love.

When you are ready to make changes for yourself, it can bring up the fear of what others think. This brings me back to my people-pleasing tendencies. What would my husband think if I started to change who I am (was I really changing who I was though or just stepping into my true self)? How would my family react if I start to put my own needs as a priority? I had a real fear over what would happen with my husband and kids if I tried to change any aspect of how I was currently living my life. I did not want to do something that would upset the current dynamic and make them love me less. Yes. I truly felt that if I changed anything about myself, including something as simple as taking care of myself, my family would not love me the same. It's easy to think that is a crazy thought but we all have things that we fear and it's not up to anyone else to try to say that they are not valid fears. So whatever fears this immediately triggered for you, I understand and I'm with you. I get it, even if you think nobody else could possibly understand the fear you have around making changes to your life, how it might affect everyone around you and what that means for you and your relationships with them. Your emotions and feelings are valid and don't ever let anyone take that away from you.

That being said, I am also here to tell you that it's up to you to make these decisions for yourself, not for anyone else, not by anyone else. Only you can make a change in your life.

Now, let me ask you, which path do you want to stay on?

P.S. This book was created to be your very own ritual. A ritual to help you no longer be a people-pleasing addict. Even if you are not a people-pleaser (or at least don't think you are), I encourage you to complete the work within here to help you break through anything that is holding you back from living the best fucking life that you 100% deserve!

Trigger Warning

I need you to be aware that this book contains topics like suicidal thoughts, generational trauma, addiction, and alcoholism. If those topics hit close to home, be ready for those to possibly bring up some "stuff" to make sure you are prepared for it. This book is about healing, for me and for you.

Journal It Out

Let's jump into this right away! Take a little time to really look at your life.

- Do you recognize any people-pleasing tendencies in your daily actions? List them out.

- What does being a people-pleaser mean to you?
- In what aspects are you currently being a people-pleaser?
- Where in your life are you people pleasing the most?
- How is that impacting you negatively?
- What would your life look like if you stopped people pleasing?
- What would your life look like if you started taking care of yourself?
- What fears are coming up for you?

One

The Breaking Point

It Bitch Slapped Me

It was springtime, the weather was finally getting warm and everything was starting to come into bloom. The trees were turning green again and the flowers were starting to come up, the world was waking up and it was beautiful. Despite all of that, I could not see the beauty. I was not able to find joy in my days. I was married to a wonderful man, my best friend. We have two beautiful and healthy children that are the center of my world, and yet, I am always sad. I cry all the time. The thoughts that run through my head are that out of a Stephen King novel. They would make Freddy Krueger cringe. This was my reality.

Every day was exactly the same. I would wake up and get breakfast for my husband and two kids, feed the dog, and start laundry because let's be honest, it never fucking ends. Time to get everyone up. Now, this may sound like no big deal, but I live with 3 people who sleep like the dead. I have literally dressed my children while they slept and carried them to the car while trying to wake them so we wouldn't be late. Next, we move onto packing lunches, cleaning up breakfast, picking up the toys or the mess the dog made, and all the other mundane shit we do to keep our houses running. This might not seem too bad to you or maybe even normal so why am I complaining? Well, let me clear that up. I am not complaining, but let me add in that I am dealing with some severe depression, undiagnosed at this time, and even getting out of bed feels like something I should be given a gold medal for, so all of these additional tasks take about every ounce of energy I can conjure up in a day. I am exhausted all the time. I am just sad all the time. I cry, ALL THE TIME. I hide it from everyone around me which adds an extra layer of exhaustion into the mix.

As the kids got older, all the extra to-do's suddenly changed. My son has played hockey since he was 3. We started on a deck and then moved to ice. We spent countless hours in the car driving to and from practices and traveling all over for games. It was an amazing experience that I will always cherish, but man, it was exhausting. My son was 5 and deep into the ice hockey life when my daughter was born, so she grew up at an ice rink. Early morning practices, and by early morning I mean like 5am be suited up and ready to go. Let's remember that at 5 years old, they are incapable of getting themselves ready. On top of getting everyone out of the house with breakfast in hand and a baby in the other arm, I also had to drag myself, the baby and the 5-year-old into the locker room to get him dressed for practice. Then my daughter and I got to sit on the benches for an hour or two until they were done, back to the locker room, undress, back in the car, and back home by 9am. Let the day begin!

Seriously though, I share this because this was my life for probably 10 years. Of course, as he got older, I no longer had to enter the sacred locker room, thank you Jesus. If you have never had the glorious opportunity of smelling a hockey bag or locker room full of hockey playing boys, count your blessings my friends because it is hideous. When my daughter got older, she started to participate in a wide variety of activities. We tried ice skating, hockey, soccer, dance, gymnastics, cheerleading, volleyball, girl scouts, t-ball, and I am certain I am missing some others in there. As you are running yourself into a rag doll with all of the sports and activities, you also have to remember to take your turn volunteering for the class parties, Parent-Teacher meetings, school snack days, science projects, class fundraising, and on and on it goes. While you are partaking in all of these activities, chances are you only concern yourself with the well-being of your children and possibly your spouse. Am I hitting too close to home? This was one of my biggest mistakes and what I would tell anyone to change immediately.

Let me give you an example. I had trouble getting out of bed on a daily basis. Depression is not only a mental issue; it drains you physically and emotionally. Everyone's symptoms are different of course, but my depression came with extreme fatigue and lack of interest in ANYTHING. However, my kid played hockey, which was his entire world, so it was my entire world. And it took up A LOT of our time. If you are not familiar with ice hockey, let me just say that early weekend games at this age was the norm. I'm talking on the ice at 6am. So that means if you have an hour drive to the rink plus the 30 minutes it takes to get them dressed and focused, you are crawling your ass out of bed at 4am to get everyone up, dressed, fed, stuffed into the minivan and on your way to the rink. This is extremely challenging for any mom. Factor in a mom suffering from severe depression and we are talking struggles of epic fucking proportions.

There was this one morning where we had to be at a rink that was 90 minutes away and ready to play at 5:45 am. My husband was working and not able to help out.

Side note, this was pretty normal. My husband worked shift work so he missed a lot. I will give my man some big-time kudos however, when he was not working, he was 100% present, active, and available in all aspects of our children's lives. He was not one to say it was my job, he was not afraid to roll up his sleeves and change diapers, wash dishes, or carry a hockey bag. Which was great, but with his job and me being the stay-at-home mom meant that most of the time it all fell on me. Let's not forget that my people-pleasing tendencies always pushed me to do everything and anything to keep my family's life easy and happy. And back to the story.

When my alarm went off, I cried. I cried because the thought of tackling everything that morning alone was so overwhelming that I didn't physically or emotionally think I could handle it. My children were not morning people, they did not get up and function on their own, at any age, and frankly, it's still a challenge for them. I finally rolled out of bed and forced myself to shower. How? I don't know honestly, the hand of God guiding me I guess since I was laying in bed crying, and praying for strength to get through the day. I have many days I don't have a clue as to how I managed through them because just getting out of bed sounded as daunting as running a marathon. My daughter was still pretty little at this point in time, so I always had a bag ready to go to practices and games filled with activities, toys, snacks, and blankets. Thankfully, that was ready to roll and all I had to do was get the kids up and out the door. The hockey bag was packed up the night before so it was also ready to go. I grabbed some breakfast they could eat in the car, coffee because it was my lifeline, and now all I had to do was get the kids. During these days, most times, I found it easier to just dress the kids while they slept and then carry them to the car. Nothing different this morning. As I got the kids packed up and everything else loaded into the car, I put myself into the driver's seat and buckled in. Time for another breakdown. I looked at the clock and realized that we were never going to make it in time. All of my breakdowns had lasted longer than I thought and obviously my movements were more sluggish I realized, because we were way behind schedule. Even if I exceeded the speed limit the entire drive, he would not be ready for the drop of the puck. He was going to be very upset with me as was the coach. Anyone else have major issues with people being upset with them? Hmm, could it be that people-pleasing addiction thing I suffer from and over volunteering as a result of it.

4

Let me add an additional little side note. I had taken on the responsibility of being the Team Mom (foolish, maybe, people-pleasing, definitely). This meant that I had the folder that contained all the player information, rosters, birth certificates, etc., all vital info that if requested, needed to be presented. Fingers crossed nothing was needed that morning until I arrived. Have you ever showed up late to something? I hate being late, but being in a state of constant depression and anxiety, it happened more than I would like. As we ran into the rink, my son was very upset with me, my daughter woke up crying, not wanting to be there, and getting looks from everyone because of course we were late again. To be fair, everyone was probably not looking at me thinking anything, this was most likely in my head due to my mental state at the time. However, I immediately wanted to break down because I was so ashamed and embarrassed. How did I allow this to become my life?

The Depression and Anxiety

I have probably suffered from both of these illnesses since childhood, just undiagnosed. Growing up in the chaos and dysfunction that I did, anxiety is the norm. I never knew it was something other than just the way things were. Looking back, I can say there was always depression underlying, I was just always very good at hiding it. That was until it became severe.

I mean I was born into a world of chaos, a world of a 16-year-old living on an army base with her husband who, based on stories I've been told, was abusive, causing her to run back home to her family. The chaos continued as she looked for something, she was always looking for a way to be complete, I'm not sure she ever found it. Anyway, I was born into chaos and the childhood that ensued, looking back, brought on trauma, depression, and anxiety. It was undiagnosed of course because there was no chance I would have ever even brought up the possibility that there was something wrong.

That went against my survival mechanism of people-pleasing. Nothing was ever about me. EVER. If I tried to make something about myself, it would turn into WW3. I learned, very early, to shove down any need that creeped in, lock it away. It was not important, it would not help you survive every day. You get up and you take care of everyone else. That is how you live your life. That is how you survive and isn't just surviving what life is all about?

And I did. That is exactly how I survived my childhood, teen years and carried it into my adult life. I kept it up into my marriage and motherhood as well, it was what I knew, it was my pattern and it worked for me so why would I change it now? I hid my depression as best I could and life would always move forward.

We all have a breaking point, some of us just never come close to it. For those who suffer from mental health issues, we tend to teeter over the breaking point edge on the regular. I've had suicidal thoughts in my life on a few occasions. When I was younger and they came up, I just shrugged them off as though I was just trying to find a way to escape my reality, never really giving them much validity. When I had achieved my dream of creating my own family, one that was safe and happy, I did not expect for those thoughts to return.

We had decided to remodel our kitchen one year. It was an extremely long process because we did all of the work ourselves. I was home alone one morning, sitting on the kitchen floor, hammer in hand, pulling up nails out of the sub-flooring. I stopped what I was doing and just stared at the hammer. Probably for about 15 minutes, just staring at the hammer. I went into a sort of trance.The thought on repeat was, can I hit myself in the temple hard enough to end it? I mean obviously since you are reading this, it didn't happen. No, I didn't try and fail, I just didn't try. I snapped out of my trance and went back to pulling up nails. I went back to shoving down my feelings, emotions, and thoughts and returned my focus on my family and what I needed to do for them.

Motherhood and marriage saved me for a while, they provided me with purpose and the desire to keep going. I knew if I did follow through with my suicidal thoughts, one of my kids or my husband would be the one to find me and that would destroy them. Being the good people-pleasing person I was, I could never do that to them. That changed of course when it got worse, when the thoughts could no longer be turned off or ignored. I was at a point where I HAD to seek help, almost forced to ask for it. I had to recognize that I could no longer pretend to be "fine." It's okay if you feel like you can't ask for help but if you are having thoughts that consume you, thoughts that would horrify if spoken out loud, it's time, FORCE yourself.

The Crumbling Edge

When I was in my late 30's, it got harder to hide. My daughter started experiencing issues at school, bullying that turned into cyber bullying. We found out she was experimenting with cutting. She had some friends that were not good influences on her. She was sneaking out, sneaking boys in her window, vaping, probably drinking (I didn't find out about actual drinking until later on), and God only knows what else was going on during those early teen years. We ended up having to pull her out of school, she switched to cyber-school and she started therapy. This entire situation was so hard on all of us. Earl and I were tested as parents (not the first time, certainly not the last). We learned even more to lean on each other, lean on our faith, and on our family. I put everything into him and into our daughter to make sure she was okay. After about 9 months or so, things began to settle down.

That is when I hit a wall. That was the moment that edge I had been standing on began to crumble beneath my feet. It was like everything I had been holding onto, shoving deep down since childhood erupted and there was no way it could be stopped. I fell into a deep, dark hole of depression. Of course, I thought I was covering it up and hiding it so good that nobody around me had a clue anything was wrong. I was certain I had mad ninja skills. I came to find out later, this was in fact false. Apparently, I suck at hiding my feelings.

I had trouble getting out of bed. I couldn't focus at work, my performance dropped, and my attitude was pretty much: "I don't give a fuck," which when your job is customer service tends to be a problem. In a meeting one day with my manager, he gently asked if I was okay. He said listening to my latest calls, my tone, my demeanor, and everything about the way I handle myself at work had changed. He provided me with some resources that the company offered to reach out for therapy. I thanked him and took the information, but I didn't really think I needed help. I've been dealing with this sort of thing my entire life all by myself and doing a bang-up job, I could keep going, I'd be fine. Yep, I'm FINE.

I continued on for a few more weeks, thinking I was OK. I was managing. I was hiding my anxiety, depression and panic attacks from everyone (ninja remember), I'd be fine. That's what moms say isn't it? I'M FINE!

Getting out of bed most days felt pointless. If I could lay in bed all day and just sleep, that's exactly what I'd do. Why did I need to get up and shower? It seemed like a stupid, non-essential task. Same with brushing my hair, my teeth, doing makeup was a joke, and wearing anything but PJ's seemed ludicrous. Things I used to enjoy like reading books, gardening, going outside, or movement of any kind all seemed like a big waste of my time. Put on the TV, it doesn't matter what it is, I didn't really pay attention to it, it was like white noise, pull the covers up and just lay in bed. Drift in and out of sleep. This is how I preferred to spend my days. I'm pretty sure after a few hours at work, laying on the floor of your office in the fetal position was normal right? I should mention that I work from home so it's not quite as awkward as it sounds. Yep. I was just fine.

Then, one day, I found myself sitting at my computer Googling "how to commit suicide to look like an accident so family gets insurance money." WTF?! Did I really just type that into a search bar? It was like an out of body experience that I couldn't even believe what I was reading. Had I had suicidal thoughts? Absolutely. Remember the hammer story? I had considered swerving into oncoming traffic in front of a big tractor trailer. I thought about grabbing handfuls of pills and going to sleep. Wondered if I'd actually be able to pull a trigger. Sorry, things got a little dark there, but yeah, the thought had crossed my mind.

People-pleasing had always saved me from suicide. Because, what always stopped me was worrying about others. I couldn't possibly do that to the driver of the tractor trailer, he'd have to live with killing someone in an accident for the rest of his life - what that would do to him. The thoughts of one of my kids finding me after overdosing on pills, or a trigger pull, or a hammer hit was more than I could do to them and their own mental health. But here I was actually Googling this shit and it was my wake up call. It was the moment that I realized that I could no longer do this alone. I did in fact, need help. While I may never believe I could act on the thoughts, the thoughts themselves needed to stop. The next day, I used the resources through my employer and called a therapist.

I began going to an office that provided both therapy and a mental health nurse practitioner who managed my medications. Working with them both, we agreed, I needed to take some time off work to get myself on a path of healing. I needed to take some "me time" and really work on getting better. This was such a new concept to me because my entire life has been all about taking care of everyone around me. I didn't really know what it meant to take "me time." It sounded like some foreign thing that only rich people or women that don't have families do. Isn't self-care just getting a massage or your nails done or taking a bubble bath? How is that going to help me at all? I don't have time for that frilly shit, I have a family to take care of. That was my first introduction to real self-care. Now, it's your turn. Here is your first REAL Self-Care Assignment. Use the following worksheets to help you identify your breaking point and recognize the signs within yourself and your body.

Journal it Out

- How are you feeling right now? Be honest my friend, nobody else is going to read this.
- Can you think of one thing you can do for yourself today? Don't get crazy, even if it's just 5 minutes of quiet time, a few minutes to read a book, take a walk outside, just a few minutes of something just for you. You need to give yourself grace and compassion. Be kind to yourself.

Resources

If you recognize you are at a breaking point and unsure what to do, here are some resources for you to turn to. Ask for my help my friend. (*I know it's a scary thought but* **TRUST** *me, it's okay and* **YOU** *deserve to receive the help you need*).

- National Suicide Prevention Lifeline, 800.273.8255; you can also text HELLO to 741741. Both services are available 24/7.
- Veterans Crisis Line, 800.273.8255 & press 1; text 838255; chat via veteranscrisisline.net ; All services available 24/7 for service members and their families.
- Domestic Violence 800.799.SAFE (7233), TheHotline.org (chat option available); Available 24/7, Confidential
- National Sexual Assault Hotline, 800.656.4573, www.rainn.org; chat online.rainn.org; Available 24/7
- BetterHelp (Online Counseling App)
- TalkLife (Mental Health Support App)
- Teladoc - Download the App or Call 800.TELADOC (835.2362); Avail-

able 24/7
- Reach out to a Religious Leader you trust
- Call a family member or friend
- Check with your employer for any EAP resources (Employee Assistance Programs), lots of employers provide them and they offer mental health resources, therapy, etc.

OK. Now What?

Carl Naumbere, Phd wrote in Psychology Today, the C.A.L.M. Method. To guide you to check in with your body and your mind. Where are you holding your stress?

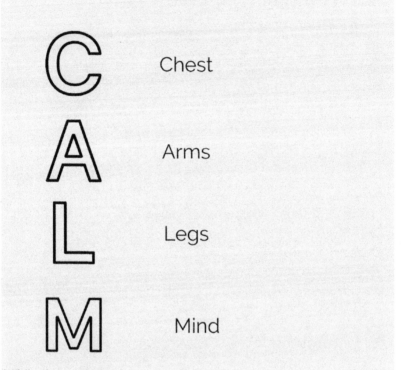

C   Chest

A   Arms

L   Legs

M   Mind

While the acronym is a good reminder to calm down and breathe, the point of it is to check in with yourself. Can you feel the stress and tension in any of these points?
Remember the point of this is recognition. ,

How to figure out if you are at your breaking point.

Recognition is the 1st and most crucial step

Do you recongize any of these signs

Changes in your sleeping habits
....

Changes in your eating habits
....

Lack of concentration, focus, feeling in a blur
....

Extra irritable or emotional
....

Less social, prefer isolation, withdrawn
....

Lack of enjoyment, happiness
....

Feelings of unworthiness
....

Suicidal thoughts
....

Your own personal sign
....

Two

Childhood

Divine Disfunction

In order for you to fully understand my desperate need for help as an adult and where the people-pleasing began, let's start way back at the beginning.

I was born at an army hospital in North Carolina at 5:55am. My mother was 17 and a long way from home. I don't know much about this time of life except that she didn't stay in NC long. As the story goes, my birth father was not a very loving husband and shortly after I was born, my mother called my grandmother to come and get her. My mother and I have never actually discussed this time period and my grandmother is no longer with us, so details are minimal. My biggest takeaway from this is the time of my birth, to me, it's significant. You see, 5:55 is an Angel Number (*Angel Number Reference Guide Available In The Resources Section*) and being born at that time has special meaning to me. To me, it signified that I was meant for greatness, I was meant to make a difference, I was divinely guided and protected. Let's pull the reins on that, I'm getting ahead of myself here. We will go into that more later. Back to my early days.

Dust Particles

I do not recall much about my early childhood. I spent some time researching issues with my memories. I couldn't understand why my husband can seem to remember everything about his childhood and I struggled to recall a handful of memories. I found an *article published in 2010 by BMC Neurology that speaks to the connection between childhood trauma and cognitive function in adults, including sporadic memory loss. It made me feel better knowing that this wasn't just a "me problem," but something that seems to be normal in adults who have suffered childhood pain and trauma. Because of this, I like to refer to my memories as "Dust Particles." They tend to show up when light is shined on them, otherwise, they stay hidden. I'm still working through all my dust particles in therapy. (Does therapy ever end, asking for a friend).

I have been told that we lived with my grandparents after they rescued us from North Carolina. When my mother and I left my grandparents, we moved in with mom's best friend. During this time is when I would connect with my best friend, the niece of mom's roommate. We always joked about being best friends since we were in diapers and it was true. We were more like sisters most of our life until I went and had a kid of my own and got married. She wasn't at that stage of her life yet and it caused us to drift apart.

My mother met husband #2 when I was pretty young and would remain married to him until I was in approximately seventh grade. This is also the time frame where my brother entered the family, he is 7 years younger than me so I was always trying to look out for him. She didn't marry again until I was an adult, but in 11th grade, we moved in with who would become husband #3.

That is a pretty big time-frame especially for our brain development and wiring with lots of happenings so let's get into some of the significant dust particles that I can remember that shaped my childhood experiences I remember we moved frequently, which meant a lot of different houses and going to a variety of schools before finally settling in a place that offered

15

some permanency.

I remember the house where I got my very first bike, a 10-speed. This was also the house that had my very favorite babysitter. I absolutely adored her. She was young and fun and I always looked forward to nights when she would come over. There were times she would have her boyfriend come, which I'm not sure it was allowed, but she didn't care. They would dance and laugh and drink Mickeys Big Mouth beer. It was pure joy and I soaked up every ounce of it.

I remember a time that we lived in a house with lots of property. This is also the place where there were fields of marijuana growing. While in this location, I can recall a time of chaos and panic, a bonfire, and talk about police coming. My mother and husband #2 were running into the house and grabbing stuff and throwing it onto the bonfire. I'm pretty sure they were lighting the fields of weed on fire also, but I can't confirm that memory 100%. I remember that my brother was a baby and I was looking after him, while also gathering up drug paraphernalia and throwing it into a big bonfire in the backyard, trying to destroy all the evidence before the cops raided the house.

I remember the place where I found out my grandmother had passed away. This was also the location where I found out that husband #2 would be going to prison. I guess creating a bonfire of all the evidence doesn't get you out of jail time.

I remember moving into a house that my mother and husband #2 actually purchased, making it the most permanent thing I had ever experienced. I had my own bedroom. My brother had his own room. There was a big yard, a swing set, it was like we were a normal happy family. I suppose for a while we were as normal as I had ever experienced. Husband #2 was out of jail, they both had jobs, my brother and I were in the same school we were in the previous year, yep, all normal here. There was still drinking, drugs and fighting, I just think I was older and escaped to my room or to a friend's house to avoid it.

The Family Inheritance

I feel like I need to give you a little more perspective on this whole situation. My mother is an alcoholic. My grandfather was an alcoholic. My biological father (husband #1), is an alcoholic. Her second husband was an alcoholic. Her latest husband is an alcoholic. **I say this as MY opinion.**

Just in case you were wondering, according to Webster's Dictionary, the actual definition of alcoholism is this:

Definition of *alcoholism*: continued excessive or compulsive use of alcoholic drinks

    2. a: a chronic, a progressive, potentially fatal disorder marked by excessive and usually compulsive drinking of alcohol leading to psychological and physical dependence or addiction

    NOTE: Alcoholism is typically characterized by the inability to control alcoholic drinking, impairment of the ability to work and socialize, tendency to drink alone and engage in violent behavior, neglect of physical appearance and proper nutrition, alcohol-related illness (such as hepatitis or cirrhosis of the liver), and moderate to severe withdrawal symptoms (such as irritability, anxiety, tremors, insomnia, and confusion) upon detoxification.

    b: acute alcohol poisoning resulting from the usually rapid consumption of excessive alcoholic beverages

The definition of being an alcoholic according to AA is: *"a distinct physical desire to consume **alcohol** beyond our capacity to control it, and in defiance of all rules of common sense"* and they always far exceeded that. If you ask any of them, they would tell you I'm full of shit. I happen to believe that when someone drinks, every single day, until they slur their words or can't stand, they are an alcoholic. If you wake up in the morning and the cure for your hangover is another beer, you're an alcoholic. If you don't see a problem with driving around with your kids drunk off your ass, you're an alcoholic. If you hide liquor outside of your house, you are an alcoholic. Alas, these are simply my opinions and nothing diagnosed by a professional.

The Mother of All Wounds

At 16 years old, I was not prepared for the day when my mother asked me to take her to find her bottle of whiskey. I don't think there is any age where you would be prepared for that sort of question. What the fuck does that even mean? Go find your bottle? Why the hell isn't it in the kitchen cabinet or down in the bar? Where exactly are we going? So many fucking questions.

This brings me to the first time that my mother asked me to go help her find her liquor. You see, husband #3, does not believe he is an alcoholic, but that my mother is. His philosophy is that if you only drink beer, you can't be an alcoholic. However, if you drink the hard stuff, you definitely have a problem. So, if my mother only drinks beer, they are cool. When she busts out the Jim Beam, he has a problem with it. To solve this little dilemma they have, she decided that she would hide her bottles of rum and whiskey in secret spots that he will never find. The problem was that she doesn't remember where she hid them either because she didn't choose to hide them in the house, but went super ninja with it and hid the bottles outside of the home. And I do mean outside of the home! We went on a search up and down back roads, looking behind rocks, dirt piles, fences, anywhere she thought she may have stashed her precious booze.

She located a few of the buried treasures, but there are still many out there waiting to be discovered, if only we had a treasure map with some x's on it!
This was a fun little activity we did on several occasions. The other mother-daughter time we spent was me driving her to her dealer's house. By this time, she had moved into just smoking weed (illegal back then, still is in this state) and left the hard stuff behind. There was truly no way for me to get

out of these joy rides. If she did not get her way, she would throw a tantrum like a 3-year-old or she would get mean, like 10x the *Mean Girls* definition of mean. Then she would bring out the victim mentality and make me the bad guy. The best way to keep her calm and happy was for me to put on my people-pleasing panties and drive her around to get her drugs and alcohol.

There were times I had come home from school to find mirrors with lines of coke on the coffee table. Crumpled aluminum foil with black tar residue inside. Rolling papers and weed particles inside of a frisbee. This was hard to explain to friends who didn't live in this sort of environment. The cocaine was left behind, to my best knowledge, when she found husband #3. Just like the beer thing, weed good, everything else bad. I don't know, it's a philosophy that I was never able to understand, but apparently worked for them.

The fact that my parents had loose morals around giving alcohol to minors became something that my friends enjoyed immensely. When I was 13, I was given wine coolers and toilet paper for my birthday. I had a few friends over for a sleepover and my mother thought it would be fun if we drank and went out toilet papering houses while sipping back on some Seagrams Berry.

When I moved back home from college, I had parties at the house and anyone could drink if you turned in your keys. Let's remember when I returned home from college, I was only 18. My friends of course thought this was the coolest thing ever and I guess most times I did too. Looking back on it now, I think it was more just them wanting to stay young, seem cool, and have people to party with.

At one of the parties, my mom decided she needed to collect money from everyone to contribute to the booze. I was so embarrassed, but what was I going to do? She certainly wouldn't stop if I asked, so she did her thing. She went around asking everyone for money, one of the guys that was not a regular grabbed a buck out of his pocket, crumbled it up and threw it at her telling her not to spend it all in one place. Disrespectful? Absolutely. Did my mother overreact, 100%. The next thing I know, her and her husband are back down in the basement with a gun in hand. I was like WTF is happening! Holding onto the gun, pointing it in the air (thankfully it was not being directed towards anyone) they "gently reminded" everyone that they were asking for donations to be put towards the purchase of the alcohol. This was before the days of cellphones or this shit would have gone viral and the cops would have certainly been knocking on our door taking some people away in cuffs.

Daddy Issues

The first time I met my biological dad I was around 12 years old. The intention was not actually to meet him, but to connect with my grandma and aunts. Unknown to me, my grandmother (dad's mom, we shall call her Grandma V) had been keeping tabs on me my entire life, but I don't believe this was really welcomed by my mother. You see, my dad did not pay child support, this was not for a lack of effort on my mother's part. She wanted her fucking money and she did everything she could to get it. My mother is one of those people who believes the world OWES her and she will do anything she has to do to claim what she believes is rightfully hers. Every effort to collect was given but when someone doesn't work, it's pretty hard to take their money, just sayin'.

As we have already discussed, my brain doesn't function at full capacity and my memories are sketchy so I'm not 100% sure who set up the get-together with my Grandma V. My first real memory was a sleepover at her trailer. She lived in this big trailer park about 20 minutes from my Aunt Sherry's house. I'm sure I met her before this because who is going to just send a kid to stay a weekend with someone they never met? I mean given all I know about my childhood; I suppose this is quite possible, but I have some dust particle memories of meeting her a few times prior to this. This just sticks out as a solid memory probably because it's the first time I met the sperm donor.

Back to the lecture at hand (did you just sing that in your head in Dr Dre's voice, no, just me, okay). I was staying with my grandmother for the weekend, she was hosting a sleepover with a bunch of kids, I'm guessing other family members and cousins, but again, a sketchy brain. I can remember my grandmother (she was a sweet and loving woman), my grandfather (didn't talk much) and two aunts who I can remember as always being very attentive and nice to me anytime I was around.

I believe it was the day I was leaving my Grandma V's, my Aunt Sherry was picking me up when I actually met him. I could tell my Grandma V was really excited for this to happen, I was super nervous, and he seemed pretty nonchalant about the entire thing. He seemed much older than my mom, shorter than I expected, and he looked like he just stepped off the field at a Grateful Dead festival. We exchanged the typical hello's and then the awkward silence set in. I mean, what exactly am I supposed to say to the father that I just met? The one whom had nothing to do with me for the first 12 years of my life? My mother would have wanted me to ask where her damn money was, but I figured that might upset my grandma. Instead, we just stood around, looking at the ground, brief glances at each other, shuffling our feet awkwardly waiting for the moment to be over. After what seemed like hours, but in reality, was probably under 10 minutes, my grandmother interrupted to say that I better go gather my stuff, my aunt would be here soon. Sigh of relief, I happily ran off to pack up my bag and wait for my aunt to arrive so she could rescue me from this strange situation.

That was how I met my dad. Fun times. Our next interaction would happen at my first full-on family function with his entire family. His baby sister was getting married. My Grandmother V really wanted me to be there so of course, I didn't want to upset her (people-pleaser remember) and agreed to it as long as it was okay with my mother. I honestly figured she would say no unless she got some sort of payment, which I suppose she may have received, but either way, I was attending a wedding. I don't remember much about the night other than I had to dance with my dad because everyone just thought it was such a great idea and a perfect time for us to bond. It was truly nothing more than weird back and forth movement in mostly silence, maybe some small talk like you would have with a stranger at a gas station.

After that night, I didn't really hear from him or see him again for at least a year, maybe longer. It was pretty hit or miss with him making contact. Nothing consistent that's for sure and I didn't actually see him again until I was around 16. We were living with husband #3 when I went to spend the day with good ole daddy. Another awkward day of him introducing me to his friends, playing the part of loving dad. I had my best pair of people-pleasing panties on that day as I smiled and joked and laughed with everyone. I sure as hell wouldn't want to upset the dad that was so reliable in my life. Mr. Reliable disappeared again after that when mom and husband #3 wanted money. I didn't see him again until I was 18 and working at a bar as a waitress. That family reunion turned into the cops being called and me never speaking to him again.

The Past is in The Past

I'd like to be all philosophical and say I wouldn't change a thing, but that would be a lie. I've done enough healing and inner work to be able to say that my upbringing and all the shit I've gone through has molded me into the person I am today. However, to say that I wouldn't like to have some different childhood memories would be a big line of shit I was trying to feed you to make it sound all fluffy. And if you haven't yet realized it, that just isn't who I am. I will always keep it real with you.

Hard to Hear Statistics

- Children of addicts are eight times more likely to develop an addiction.
- A 1985 study suggests a strong genetic component, particularly for the onset of alcoholism in males. Sons of alcoholic fathers are four times

more likely to become alcoholics.

- The use of substances by parents and their adolescent children is strongly correlated. Generally, if parents use drugs, sooner or later their children will as well.
- Children who use drugs are more likely to have one or more parents who also use drugs.
- Children of addicted parents experience greater physical and mental health problems and higher health and welfare costs then do children from non-addicted families.
- A child who perceives that a parent is more permissive about the use of drugs is more likely to use drugs themselves.
- These statics are reported by Orlando Recovery Center at https://www. orlandorecovery.com

Resources for Help

Al-Anon - https://al-anon.org, 1-888-4AL-ANON

Alcoholics Anonymous - https://www.aa.org

The Complete ACOA Sourcebook by Janet Geringer Woititz, Ed.D

Journal It Out

- Are you suffering from wounds inflicted from your childhood? Physical or Emotional?
- This is the time to write down the pain and trauma you are carrying from your past. Recognizing what you are holding onto is the first step to healing.
- Do you recognize that you could have an addiction of your own?
- How does it feel to admit it?

*Majer, M., Nater, U.M., Lin, JM.S. *et al.* Association of childhood trauma with cognitive function in healthy adults: a pilot study. *BMC Neurol* 10, 61 (2010). https://doi.org/10.1186/1471-2377-10-61

Learn To Identify

The Complete ACOA Sourcebook is a book that I highly recommend to anyone who believes they may fall within the parameters of an ACOA (Adult Children Of Alcoholics). Whether you yourself are dealing with addictions or are trying to heal the pain and trauma you experienced in your childhood as a result of addict parents, this book is extremely beneficial. She lists 13 characteristics that are common in ACOA that I'm going to share with you, if they resonate with you, you will have a better understanding of what is going on and why. I recommend getting her book, she goes into great detail of each characteristic, what they mean and their implications.

- You guess at what normal is

- You have difficulty following a project through from beginning to end

- You lie when it would be just as easy to tell the truth

- You judge yourself without mercy

- You have difficulty having fun

- You take yourself very seriously

- You have difficulty with serious relationships

- You overreach to changes which you have no control over

- You constantly seek approval and affirmation

- You feel you are different from other people

- You are either super responsible or super-irresponsible

- You are super loyal even when it isn't deserved

- You are impulsive which can lead to self-loathing or loss of control

Three

Monkey See, Monkey Do

How The Fuck Did I Become My Parents

I was 17 years old when I started college. What the hell did I know at this point in my life? I knew that I was finally out of my parents' house. I was free. I was as happy as I ever remember myself being. This was my chance to really be myself. This was my chance to shape my future. I was going to do better, be better than my parents. That was my plan. Sometimes things don't go as planned.

On my first day at school, I was informed I would be in a room alone. No roommate. I was both happy about this and sad all at the same time. I didn't have to worry about being paired up with someone who would drive me crazy. At the same time, I was also craving friendship, so I was disappointed that I wouldn't get the chance to bond with a new roommate.

In the elevator while moving in, I met my first new friend. We hit it off immediately and we remain friends to this day. The girls in the room right beside me were childhood friends of each other and we all became fast friends. I am still in contact with the friends I made during my year at school to this day. While I don't see them much or even truly get to talk to them often because we are spread all over the country, I treasure the connection we made that year. We had so much fun together, they showed me true love

26

connection, and sisterhood, when I needed it most.

I went into my freshman year wanting to be a nurse. I had to take a test to get into the program. I was ready, or so I thought. My Aunt Sherry drove down to school the day of the test to take me over to the testing site at the hospital. I went in with confidence, I was so certain I would be able to get through this test and be accepted into the nursing program. By the time I left the hospital that day, my confidence had slipped in a big way. It was much harder than I ever expected. When I got the notice that I did not make it into the program, I was at a loss for what to do next.

I had to change my major to something else or keep it what it was and hope for better results next year. I decided to go into General Studies until I could figure out what to do with my life. My class schedule stayed the same and I struggled. I was in chemistry and biology, pre-reqs for the Nursing Program. As my confidence in my ability to get into the program continued to diminish, so did my ability to understand the classes. Perhaps it was more a lack of my ability to want to understand or to even put any effort into trying. I was going to my classes, but I half-assed it all the way.

Cue The Limiting Beliefs

This was triggering all the bullshit beliefs that had been fed to me all my life. All of the beliefs that I had about myself, what I thought was my truth.

- You're not good enough
- You're not smart enough
- You will never make anything of yourself
- You are trailer trash
- You will be a drunk nobody just like your parents

Limiting beliefs are a bitch, they become that nasty voice that lives in your brain and repeatedly tells you what you can't do, what you should believe, what you shouldn't, what actions you should take and what you shouldn't.

These are just a few of the limiting beliefs that I let takeover on the day I took my nursing exam. The things that others had said to me all of my life that for the most part lived in a little vault inside my brain. However, that day they all came pouring out in full force. I hadn't given them much weight in the past, but that day they became significantly stronger. I started to believe them. At this point in my life I had No clue that these thoughts were just beliefs, some of them not even my own. It wouldn't be until much later that I would begin to learn about these beliefs that were running my life in ways and areas that I hadn't even realized.

The Party Girl

What I did put all of my effort into was going out and having fun with my friends. At first, it was just us going out and having fun on a Friday or Saturday night. Learning all about college life and freedom from our parents. It wasn't until I realized my future was uncertain after the fateful day of the nursing exam that I went full on Party Girl. Figuring out where the best party of the night was going to be became my main focus. What frat I should hang out at that night was more important than the homework I had or the test I should be studying for the next day.

I became a full-on party girl. Keep in mind I had just turned 18 at this point. I knew all of the Frat houses, what nights they had which type of party, and I got to know a lot of the main party circles of people. I would walk into a party and head straight for the keg. Keg stand anyone? Beer Bong? Yep, been there, done that. My friends would go to the parties with me most nights. Most of them were still very invested in school and their education so some nights they were not into the party scene. I made enough connections at parties that I always had someone to go out with. A few months in, I was spending so much time at a particular Frat that they asked me to pledge as a "little sister" and hell yeah, I was in! I spent more and more time in the house and with my pledge sisters, a new group of party people. Looking back on it, I think it was more than just a group to party with, it was a family type atmosphere where I was wanted and accepted. I was part of something. It felt good to be wanted, to be included, to always have somewhere to go where I wouldn't be judged or criticized constantly. It was that type of inclusion that I craved for years and would continue to crave and search for long after leaving school.

I became an official little sister after going through the obligatory hell week and hell night. Hell night was pretty much what you hear about. In a dark, damp basement being yelled at, made to drink or eat nasty shit, smacked with the frat paddles and then once it's all done, you are celebrated as a member of the family. You hug your "bigs" and your pledge brothers and sisters and then you drink until you puke. My drink of choice was not only beer, but Blue Hawaiian schnapps mixed with 7-up, don't judge it was the 90's. As my big sister held my hair that night, the toilet was blessed with a shit ton of blue puke. This was the first of many such nights.

Another thing I discovered at college was that boys found me attractive or at the very least appealing enough to have sex with. Now, as an adult looking back, I realize that pretty much anything with a pulse is enough appeal for most college boys. To the 18-year-old me that was searching for love, acceptance and attention, this felt amazing. So much in fact, that I took full advantage of all the attention I received from the opposite sex. This is an area that I would like to go back and tell my younger self to knock that shit off. I didn't need to find my worth in their bed. I needed to love myself so deeply that their pathetic and empty words actually meant nothing, but this is one of those lessons I had to go through to learn. I hopped from guy to guy, bed to bed, seeking something for where it could never be found.

I remember one night at a party, a friend and I made a bet at who could kiss more guys. Yep, that's an actual bet we made. The prize? Bragging rights I guess. Is that really a prize? The prize actually should have been an award to the person with the lowest self-esteem, but again another one of those life lessons. Anyway, I was determined to win this little game of ours and made my way through the party, drunk off my ass, seeking out anyone that would kiss me. Not too many guys, especially drunk guys, will turn you away when you offer up a no strings attached kiss. I'm pretty sure I was way more into this game than the friend I made the bet with because I won, with flying colors.

My friends went out with me pretty regularly, but then there were nights where they actually cared about getting an education and stayed in to study. Me, not so much. I went to class most days, did the smallest amount of work possible, failed most of my tests, even fell asleep in a few classes. At night, I was the star student. I knew how to party and I knew how to get a guy to take me home. I even went out without my crew at times. Sometimes I would convince someone to go with me and then they would want to leave, but I wanted to stay, so they would head back to the dorms and I'd stay at the party.

The thing about college was, you didn't have to wait for the weekends to have a party, you could pretty much find one any night of the week. This was also another appeal to joining a Frat as a Little Sister, you could always go hang out at the house and someone would absolutely be partying. I spent many nights in the bathrooms at the dorm puking my guts out and that never seemed to deter me from giving it another go the next night. There were a few nights where I don't even remember how I made it home from the frat house or from a party somewhere. When I think back to this time I cringe at my behavior and the unsafe situations I put myself in.

Scared Straight, Nah, Just Scared Shitless

One of the scariest moments was when I thought I was pregnant. Yep, it was inevitable with the amount of sex I was having that I would encounter this scare. I have not yet mentioned this, but my older cousin went to the same school as me. He had an off-campus apartment and a roommate and I spent a lot of time at his place as well. When the scare happened, I of course turned to him for help. We found a clinic close-by that offered up testing so I made an appointment and he drove me along with his friend that I had been sleeping with at the time. I skipped out on a Bio exam because this biology was way more important than the exam I was bound to fail anyway since I didn't study a minute for it. At the clinic, I was so nervous I could have thrown up, no alcohol required. I went through the obligatory steps of peeing on a stick and then sitting and waiting for my future to be decided by a plus or minus sign. When I was provided the news that I was NOT pregnant, I cried with relief. I jumped into my cousin's arms for a big hug and the doctor performing the test gave us the evil eye. I didn't feel the need to inform him that he was wrong in his assumption, it didn't matter, he already formed an opinion of me and it wasn't worth my time to try and change it.

It was time to celebrate. We headed to the car, turned on some Stone Temple Pilots and headed back to the apartment to have a party thanking the good Lord above for having enough sense to save his precious gift for later in my life. Now, you would think that this sort of situation would make me slow down with my promiscuous ways, right? I was not a smart young lady at this time, so my logic was to just not have sex with that particular person any longer. It was time to move on and make sure I was safer next go round.

Now, I did eventually start dating someone exclusively. He was older, he was a brother at the frat and he was a genuinely good guy who actually cared about me. He had an off-campus apartment and I started spending most of my time there and with him instead of partying. This was a good thing. He came home with me at Christmas break and then I went to his house for New Years. It was a real relationship and it was nice. Until it wasn't. We got to a point where, with him being older, he wanted more and I wasn't in a position to give him what he needed. I was 18, I wanted to go out with my friends, I wanted to be reckless. He wanted a serious girlfriend, who didn't care about spending time with her friends, and who wanted to start a path of settling down. As much as I liked him and as wonderful as he was, I was not at that point in my life. I needed to let him go find what he was looking for, so we ended it.

That meant, I was back to my old tricks of going out, getting drunk, and hooking up. This pretty much went on for my entire stay on campus from 1993-1994. When May of '94 rolled around, my college years would officially become a thing of my past, an experience I paid a lot of money to have. You see, I was able to go to school only because I had received enough federal grant money that the student loans I took out didn't require any assistance from parents. When I put partying and having fun above learning, I flunked out of too many classes and lost those grants. This is another one of those moments where I wish I could go back and talk to my 18-year-old self to tell her how all this real-world shit actually works but again, life lessons.

School was out and I was heading back home. The only thing that made this bearable was a friend and I were going to spend the summer together. We had applied to work at an amusement park for the summer and both got hired. We packed up our dorms and left school, heading to my parent's house for a few days before going to the amusement park for our summer jobs but they were a bust. We both hated the positions we received and were miserable. The thoughts of spending the entire summer here made us both want to crawl into a fetal position and cry so we did what any responsible adult does, we quit and went back home. My friend decided to spend the summer at my house with me before she returned to school in the fall. We both got a job at a local retail store so we had some funds for our summer fun. We swam, had parties, worked, and hung out with new work friends. It was a good summer. With having a guest in the house, my parents kept themselves somewhat controlled with their craziness so that helped me survive living back at home.

When she left for school, it really hit home how bad I had screwed shit up, but there was nothing more to do at this point except to move on. I really started to see WAY TOO much of my parents in my current behavior and realized I needed to stop. I always knew that I would not be able to live in that house without my friend as a shield so plans needed to be made. It was time to start figuring out what the fuck I was going to do with my life.

Journal It Out

Let's look at your limiting beliefs. These are the "mean girl" things that you say to yourself. These are all of the beliefs that you hold true and stop you from achieving your dreams. They could be focused around yourself, your looks, your talents, abilities, your finances, your health, your career, any aspect of your life. Make a list of all the "beliefs" that are limiting your capability to be the person you were meant to be. Come back to the list and write them down as they come up. Knowing they exist and what they are will be how you begin to work through them and BUST THE SHIT OUT OF THEM!

Now What?

You are probably wondering what the hell you are supposed to do with all of the shit you just journaled out right?

I'm so glad you asked. Now, we are going to begin the process of reframing these bullshit beliefs. We want to find what **YOUR** true, core beliefs are, not all the lies that others have filled your head with. You need to connect with what you believe, what you value, what is actual **TRUTH** to you.

The first step in that is going to be reframing each limiting belief that you wrote down so that it feels more true, more in line to what you actually believe or at least what you want to believe.

Let me give you an example using one of my beliefs.

"You will be a drunk nobody like your parents" which I have reframed into "Because you came from alcoholic parents, you have recognized that is not the future you want for yourself, you are allowed to want more for yourself" Get the idea? Great, now it's your turn.

33

Busting Beliefs

Working through your limiting beliefs and rewiring them can take some time. It starts with awareness, here are a few tips to get you started.

1 Awareness is Key. When you hear that voice in your head telling you something negative, write it down. You have to acknowledge the limits to rework them.

2 Once you begin to write them down as they come up, you can then shift into where they came from. Your childhood, society, yourself, trauma?

3 How are these beliefs serving you? Are they keeping you safe, playing small, invisible, protection, are they holding you back?

4 If you recognize that the belief is no longer serving you, you need to let it go. Easy right? Not so much but you can do it. Start small with the reframe.
EX: I am bad with money. Reframe: I am learning to manage money better.

5 Don't give up. It takes time to change something that has been with you for years. Patience.

Four

Growing Up and Getting Out

Childhood Haven

I spent most of my childhood trying to escape my life at home, seeking refuge anywhere I could. I would spend as much time as I could at my Aunt Sherry's house and also with friends. I had a few friends who understood what life was like at home and their homes became sanctuaries for me.

Let me give a little backstory on the people in my early life who showed me that another way was possible. I have three aunts that are the sisters of my mother. The oldest, Aunt Sally, lives out of state. The other two live directly beside each other, my Aunt Jo and my Aunt Sherry. On occasion in childhood, I would spend a few weeks of summer vacation with my Aunt Sally. I would also spend weeks at a time with my Aunt Sherry and Uncle Bob, they became surrogate parents to me. During the school year, I would escape to their house on the weekends. There were two instances of them coming to our house and convincing my mother that I needed to go stay with them for a while, and let her have time to do whatever it was she did when I wasn't with her. I'd like to say get her shit together, but that is not something I ever witnessed. During the times when I stayed with Aunt Jo and Aunt Sherry, I'd rotate between houses because they lived directly beside

35

each other. It was a different school district so everyone took turns driving me to school - aunts, uncles, cousins.

There were times when during the week I'd stay with friends so we didn't have to have people drive me. I was fortunate to have a few friends whose parents were amazing humans to allow me to live with them during the week, take care of me, feed me, and provide me a safe haven to go to school and to be a kid.

I had three friends who were instrumental in providing me refuge during this time. Their families were so welcoming and allowed me to stay with them for days, even a week at a time during the school week. I'm not sure I realized just how monumental this was both for me as a child, but also from the adult perspective. Allowing someone else's child to basically live with them was a big undertaking and I will forever be grateful for what they provided, a safe space.

I was always looking for that safe haven. Somewhere I could just be me and not have everyone expecting something from me. I was searching for love and acceptance. When I was younger, I did this through friends and their families. As we have learned from the previous chapter, when I was older, I often sought this out in the beds of men. When I was 18, I was convinced I had found my savior.

The One. Or So I Thought

It was the fall of '94, after my short stint away at college. I had been working at a department store over the summer with my college friend who spent the summer with me. She left to go back to school and I was stuck at home with my mother and husband #3. My circle of friends was small. I needed more money, more friends, and more time out of the house. I started looking for a new job and landed a waitressing job at a local bar/restaurant. Just what I needed.

As I was walking through the kitchen on orientation day, I met the man who would become my husband. As I expressed interest in him, I was informed that he was dating someone. Alright, no big deal, moving on. I started to make a group of friends at work, some my age, some older, it was wonderful. One of the other waitresses was soon becoming a great friend. She was older and perhaps I looked at her as a mother figure, but I loved spending time with her and being around her. She was strong and independent; she didn't take shit from anyone, but she was also very kind and giving. Her husband was a cook at the restaurant, as was his son. I'm sure you can imagine what happened next. You guessed it, her stepson and I started dating.

After we had been dating for a while, maybe 4-5 months, shit went south at home. It was harder and harder to deal with my mother and husband #3. They were increasingly controlling, volatile, and uncompromising. I'd had enough and had to get out. One of the girls I worked with at the bar was moving out of her apartment and said she would probably be able to help me get the lease. I was able to afford it so it was a big YES. I put on my big girl panties instead of the people-pleasing ones and got my own apartment. It was scary as hell but also fucking liberating. I moved out of my parents' house before the apartment was ready so I stayed with my boyfriend (we will call him James) and his parents for a few weeks until I could move into my own place.

Once I moved in, James spent quite a bit of time there. He didn't officially live with me, but it was pretty close, except for the paying the bills part. After a few months, the landlord caught on and wanted more money. This didn't sit well and after a few more months, we decided to move out and moved in with James's sister and her boyfriend.

Things were good. I completely loved his family, loved him, loved our life. I felt certain we would end up getting engaged. We were together for about a year, then all of a sudden (or at least sudden to me) it was over. He went to a wedding without me one weekend and after that decided he no longer loved me or wanted to be with me. Done. Just like that. Over a year together wiped out in one weekend. I was devastated. In the moment my heart shattered because I was losing him, our relationship, and the future I thought we had. Looking at it now, maybe I was more crushed over losing the family I gained when we were together. His dad and step-mom were so special to me as were his two sisters, losing them was another level of the breakup that was crushing my heart.

The heartbreak also triggered my people-pleasing addiction and brought up all the stories that I carried around with me:

- If you would have been a better girlfriend, he wouldn't have left.
- You didn't do enough to keep him happy.
- You don't deserve happiness.
- You are not worthy of love.
- You will never be good enough for anyone.

Heartbreak shines a light on our inner wounds. It shows us our deepest beliefs about our worth and value. We torture ourselves with questions like the ones that were triggered in me:

- What is wrong with me?
- Am I not good enough?
- Why was I rejected?
- Why did he abandon me?
- What can I do to get his love back?
- What parts of me should I fix to earn his love back?

These questions don't serve us and we often come up with answers that make us feel ashamed and guilty. We start to conclude that we are undeserving, that it is valid for a love to leave us, that we need to work really hard to win back that love, that our value and self-worth are dependent on others. (p.s. it's not!)

At the moment we were in pain, we are ugly crying, we don't understand what happened, we are doubting every single thing about ourselves, and that is ok. It's part of the process that you must go through to heal. The key is once you come out the other side, can you find the lessons within the heartbreak. If you look at your heartbreak closely, it's actually a gift because it reveals how much or how little you love who you are. Self-love is not about identifying all the traits that make you imperfect, fixing them, and deciding that now you love yourself. It's about looking deeply within and finding gratitude for what you have and what you are in the moment.

I know, I know, you are probably rolling your eyes at me and I get it. This might seem like crazy talk or far out of reach for you right now. I'm here to tell you IT'S OKAY! Getting to a point where you can look at the pain or trauma you have experienced and then use it to help you heal can feel overwhelming. It might even sound like a big can of bullshit. I can share this with you now after years of doing the work but when I was living through it, I would have never imagined it was something that would help me learn to love myself.

Put The Shackles Back On

After the breakup, I had no choice but to move back in with my mother and husband #3. Just when I thought I was free, I felt like I had been thrown back into a dungeon. I thought moving back home after college was hard, phew, that was nothing compared to what this felt like.

I was an actual adult. I had a full-time job. I had an apartment; I paid my bills. I knew what it was like to take care of myself. Going from the freedom of doing whatever the fuck you want to being treated like a child who needs to ask permission for everything was soul shattering. I was dragged right back into my old patterns, my old habits of needing to keep them happy, to keep them calm, and avoiding any type of confrontation or chaos at all costs. I was 8 years old again.

I was not only trying to recover from a heartbreak, but now I had to try and relinquish my self-sufficiency and go back to my people-pleasing ways. It felt like no matter how many steps forward I was making in my life, something was always happening to drag me back into the shit, taking me back more steps than I could take forward. I couldn't seem to make any real progress in my life. I had no idea where to go from this point or how to get there. I felt like I was barely treading water and there was absolutely no way I would be able to sustain it.

By this time, I was no longer working at the bar/restaurant where James and I worked together. I was at a different bar working as a bartender and waitress, working pretty much all nights which was helpful in getting me away from my mother and husband #3. During the days', I would sleep and then get up and go to work. I had my friend group from my previous job and still hung out with most of them even though most were mutual friends with James. When there were parties being thrown, I wouldn't go if he did. When I wasn't working, I was always looking for somewhere to go and hang out so I didn't have to be at home. I needed to free myself from them before I was completely sucked into their chaos.

Knight In Shining Armor

At one of the parties hosted by a mutual friend, Earl, the man I met on orientation day so long ago, and I reconnected. We had always been friends, but in a casual sense, not that we actively sought each other out to hang out. It was summertime, we were hanging out at a friend's bonfire party and we found each other. We spent the night together talking, drinking, laughing, relaxing, and having fun. Two of our friends decided they wanted to go out, just to meet each other that night. They were hesitant to have a first date and asked us to double. It was a no brainer to me! Hell yeah, I've wanted to go on a date with this man for a year and a half now! We decided that the 4 of us would go on a double date so that our friends would feel comfortable getting to know each other.

That double date fell through after our friends decided they no longer needed us to be a part of their first date. That however, did not stop my knight from continuing with our date. Let's remember friends, this was the age PRIOR to everyone having cell phones. Coming out of work a few nights after the party, I saw a note on my car windshield. It was from Earl letting me know to call him so we could plan our date. My man, the romantic.

A few nights later, he picked me up in his shiny new Chevy truck and we headed to a State Park to hike along the river. After that, we went to his favorite Italian restaurant for dinner. Since we were having such an amazing time and didn't want the night to end, we headed to the drive-in for a movie. It was the best first date in the history of first dates, just sayin', I was hooked.

We were pretty much inseparable after that night. When we weren't working, we were together. At that point, I truly didn't care what my mother and husband #3 thought or said, nothing would have stopped me from spending every free minute with this man.

I just needed to figure out how to not screw everything up. I would use my people-pleasing tenancies for good not evil and I would make this work. I would finally get out of the land of dysfunction, permanently.

Journal it Out

- Do you find yourself repeating patterns in your life?
- What steps can you take to make shifts in your life to disrupt these destructive patterns?

How to break free of negative patterns

Tips to releasing habits and patterns that no longer help or serve us.

1 Define the behavior you want to change

2 Identify the triggers that keep you in these patterns and habits.

3 Accountability. Once you recognize the triggers, you need to accept responsibility around how you react to these triggers.

4 Plan. You need to determine how you are going to handle the trigger when it happens. EX: Negative pattern is coming home from work stressed everyday. Plan: Sit in the car and meditate or listen to music for 10 min before going in house.

5 Affirmation. Use them as reminders to help you break the patterns, allowing you to check in with yourself as support.

Five

Knocked Up

Oh Baby

I was spending as much time with Earl as I possibly could to escape my reality of living with my mom and husband #3. I spent much more time at his house than I had him come to mine. We went to parties with friends, we went to amusement parks, and we sat in his truck and kissed until our lips were red and puffy. I did not want to be away from him so it's no wonder that after 4 months of dating, I was pregnant.

I had just turned 21 when I found out I was pregnant. I had only been dating Earl for about 4 months. Granted, we had been friends for years prior to dating, but had only been officially a couple for a short time. To say that I was scared was an understatement, but at the same time, I had previously been told I may never have children so it was also a blessing. I had to tell him, but how could I? Telling my mother and her husband was an even scarier thought, it was not going to go well. After a trip to the doctor to solidify what a few home pregnancy tests already told me, I had to face facts, it was not something I would be able to hide for long. My people-pleasing habits were triggered big time. I was a 21-year-old girl, living in a house of alcoholic

44

control freaks who felt they could control all aspects of my life. My boyfriend was 20, living at home with his parents, and happy as could be. How could I possibly tell them all what was going on and be able to keep them all happy at the same time? I was now filled with anxiety over how to break the news and be a people-pleaser all intermixed into one.

Sharing My Big News

I told him on a phone call. Not my best moment, but it seemed the safest at the time. Shocked might not be a strong enough emotion for what he was probably feeling. The thing that I remember the most about the conversation was a few comments about "ruining his life and the biggest mistake." I was of course hurt, but I also can look back now and know that he was trying to process a huge bomb that I dropped on him. I'd had my own time to work through it, this was his time and who was I to say what the right or wrong way to do that was?

As he was working through this major shift in his life path, it was time for me to tell my parents. If I haven't already established this in previous chapters, the term parents is a very loose interpretation of what I was dealing with at home. I had to tell my mother and husband #3 the news. It was not going to go over very well at all. Despite my age, I was still living with them and they didn't give a shit that I was an adult. In their world, I was still a child living with them who they could control.

I told my mother first, and as expected, happiness was not the reaction I received. The worst of it came when husband #3 got involved in the conversation. There was no way they were going to let this happen. There was no way we would make it work. We were too young, we hadn't been together very long, we were broke, and we had no place to live because we sure as hell weren't living with them. I couldn't possibly be a mother and they would "take care of it." He was in a fit of rage, yelling, screaming, and swearing, then she started in too. I was scared and crying. I decided to leave the house because as I mentioned before, I'm an adult and don't have to put up with this shit. Now, unfortunately for me at this time, I did not have my own vehicle. Leaving wasn't that simple. I called Earl to please come rescue me and he was on his way. I told them I was leaving, which of course only added fuel to the already raging bonfire that was happening in the house. I quickly packed a bag and got out of the house and started walking towards the direction my white knight would be coming to get me.

As I was walking down a two-lane, back country road in the darkness, headlights came up behind me, so I moved a little further into the grass on the side of the road. The car stopped and the door opened, it was husband #3. He had come to take care of this baby bullshit, one way or another, he would make me lose that baby. He grabbed me and tried to shove me into the car. We struggled and fought for a while before he won, got me into the car, and drove me back to the house all while we were in a screaming battle. He dragged me into the house and they continued their berating back and forth at me. Then they started to attack each other, then back at me, and on and on this goes. When their attention turned on each other, I made another escape out of the house. This time I was full-on sprinting down the road before they realized I was gone. I needed to get as far away as I could.

Let me also add in here that this was before cell phones were mainstream, so I had no way to communicate what was happening with Earl during this chaos. I was running down the road and when I saw headlights, I jumped into bushes to hide. When I saw a car coming from the other direction, I looked out to see that it was Earl's sister's car. I jumped out of the bushes to wave them down. Once I was safely inside and we were headed back to their house, I broke down and told them what was going on. We drove back to their house (I mean their parents' house) mostly in silence. I finally felt safe and that is what was most important. I would do anything, including putting my own life at risk, to save the baby I was carrying.

Taking A Stand

Do you know what it's like to always be living in fear of what can happen if you say or do something wrong? I constantly felt like I was on egg-shells that if I did something that didn't please someone, I was going to suffer the repercussions of my actions, even if I didn't feel those actions deserved any type of backlash? For me, I had a hard time handling chaos, yelling, and anyone being "unhappy" with me. This was from my years and years of secluding myself in the bubble of people-pleasing. It was a safety net of sorts that protected me from having to deal with confrontation. I never had to stick up for myself because what I wanted didn't matter. If I lived in my bubble, most of the time I was safe.

Then something changed. This light bulb moment, this thing that happened that caused such a pull in my soul, I felt so deeply and passionately about it that it changed my course. I could have continued down the path of self-destruction, of people-pleasing, of drugs, alcohol, and sex, but instead I chose the love that was growing inside of me. I made the decision to allow my love for my unborn child to be stronger than my fear of my mother or my addiction to people-pleasing. I was going to stand up to them for the safety of my baby.

I say it like it was an easy thing. Like I flipped a switch and changed my thinking, my entire way of being with the snap of my fingers. I wish change was this easy my friend, but it's not. It takes strength and courage to do something different, to completely re-arrange everything you have ever known. It is, however, completely worth it, when you find something that you are passionate about. I was so in love with my unborn child, I was going to figure it out.

Marie Forleo says *"Everything is Figureoutable."* Back when I was making these big girl moves, I was not aware of this. I just recently read her book, which is ah-maze-balls by the way! She speaks truths, when you truly want something, you find a way to figure out how to make it happen. For me, this meant creating a boundary to keep my baby safe. I had no clue how to be a good mom, I had no role model teaching me how to set healthy boundaries, I didn't even know what the fuck that meant at the time. What I did know was that I was going to protect my baby no matter what the consequences were to me. I was going to stand up for myself and this baby, somehow, I would figure out a way to do it.

A Fresh Start

After that night of running away from home, I stayed with Earl at his parents' house for a few weeks. They had their apprehensions about their 20 year-old son becoming a father with someone he had only been dating a few months. However, they were providing as much support as they could while they worked through their feelings on their own. Things settled down enough at home that I went back there for Christmas. In January, I moved out for good this time. It was one of the most liberating experiences of my life. I knew that no matter what happened, I would never go back there. If things didn't work out with Earl, I would find a way to make it work for me and my baby. I would not put either of us back into the toxic environment that I fought so hard to get out of.

Earl and I moved into an apartment. It was a small place, one bedroom, one big room that contained a kitchen and living room and a bathroom. It was small, it was cozy, and it was all we needed for the time being. We were happy in our little apartment. We had one car we shared, but we made it work. Our places of employment were right beside each other so that helped. When he worked daylight, we ended our shifts at the same time. When he worked 3-11, I would walk over and get the car after my shift and then go pick him up when he completed his shift at work. When he worked at midnight, I'd take him to work and then he would drive home after his shift and I had a sweet woman I worked with that would give me rides when I needed them.

We made it work. That's what you do when you are "adulting" right? You figure shit out with what resources you have available to you. We didn't have much support from my "parents," but we were okay with that. We had love and support from his family and from my aunt Sherry and uncle Bob whom I consider to be essentially my true parents.

Labor Time

As far as pregnancies go, I had a pretty easy one with my first baby. No complications, nothing crazy, no insane sickness, it was standard. Mostly excited new-mom with sporadic moments of misery, swollen feet, aching back, and wanting this thing inside of me out, but you know, mostly happy expecting mom.

They decided they were going to induce me, so the date was set and I couldn't wait for it to be over. July 17th, early morning, we checked into the hospital, pretty sweet digs for a delivery room. We were so young and naïve; we had no idea what was coming. It was just us when we were checking in, then later came his parents and my aunt and uncle. Even later than that came my mother, I think her husband was there, I can't remember. I was only allowed two people in the room with me so it was Earl and Aunt Sherry. When my "mother" came, she kicked my aunt out of the room to be in there. Now, I was way too distracted with what was happening downtown to even care what was happening around me with the drama of my mother (drunk off her ass, smelling horrendously of alcohol, by the way) kicking my sweet aunt out of the room.

This labor was intense shit and this kid of mine did not feel the need to come out into the drama induced world. Nothing was working to get this kid out, Earl was getting woozy. The nurses were very concerned with his well-being and had to get him a chair to make sure he was okay. Um Hello, I'm okay over here laying in this bed, sweating my ass off, in the worst pain of my life, trying to push a fucking Mac truck out of my vagina! Yes, please make sure he doesn't pass out.

Finally, it was time for them to break out the big guns and use suction. When that wasn't working, he broke out the forceps. Holy Mother of God. You want to talk about pain. That made me scream bloody murder, my screams made hairs curl in rooms 5 doors down. After hours and hours of suction, forceps, pushing, at 11:47pm, he arrived. Our little conehead. He was gorgeous and wrinkly and covered in white goo. He had big red marks so close to his eyes from the forceps and his poor little head did in fact look like Beldar from The Coneheads. He was perfect. He was named after his dad, who was named after his dad, who was named after his dad. If you are counting, yes, we are in fact royalty and our child is the 4th.

After a few nights in the hospital, it was time to go home. Just the 3 of us to see if we could figure out this parenting shit. Back in those days, we had friends who would come visit all the time. See, we were still young and most of our friends were still single and enjoying their twenties with nothing better to do so they would always drop by our place. Our first day home, Earl's two best friends came over to see our amazing creation. It was a beautiful moment, bringing our baby boy home. Until it was time to change his diaper for the first time. The hospital sent us home without anything to tend to his poor little circumcised penis. While my man and his friend went to the local store for supplies, I had to hold my little man, diaper-less so it didn't stick to said circumcised penis.

So, there we are, me and my sweet little baby boy, sitting on the rocker, him wrapped in a soft little blanket (careful not to let it stick to, well you know) and he decided it was a good time to show me how much he loved me. Yep, he shit all over the place. Not normal shit either. It was black tar. Now, I had no clue so of course and I was freaking the fuck out. My sweet little baby has black tar flying out of his ass, this can't possibly be normal. Oh, but it was. Thankfully, one of my best friends was left behind to supervise me and the baby so he was there to help. Maybe not so much help as standing off to the side dying of laughter. But he was able to get me some towels and baby wipes, so I guess that's something. This has become a story that is told often with snorting laughter ensuing.

We lived in our tiny little apartment with the baby for a few months. Then Earl's parents decided to move to a new house and offered to sell us their old house. It was an easy decision because they were being so good to us with the offer, we happily and graciously accepted. We moved into the house at the end of 1997, just in time to have our first Christmas together.

Life was moving along, we were adjusting to being parents and doing a bang-up job of it. We were blessed that his mom was our babysitter because I had to go back to work after just 6 weeks off (which is bullshit by the way, all maternity leave should be a minimum of 3 months, just sayin'). It was hard, but dropping him off to his grandmother every day made it a little easier. We were chugging along building our life together and it was good.

Trigger Me Baby

When you are an addict, it's easy to replace one addiction with another. When you drink, you replace it with smoking. When you do drugs, you replace it with gambling. When it's sex you replace it with knitting. When it's people-pleasing, you replace it with......I have no fucking clue. I don't really have a clue about the other ones either, just spit-balling here. What I do know is that I thought I was breaking my people-pleasing tendencies whenever I placed boundaries around my mother. I was freeing myself from always feeling like I had to worry about what others were feeling and doing and saying in order to be able to determine how I was going to be feeling, doing, and saying.

Funny thing is, becoming a mom brought a whole new set of people-pleasing triggers. These were all centered around my baby and my family.

- You are gonna fuck this kid up.
- You have no clue what you are doing.
- You have never been taught any skills to help you be a good mom.
- There is no time for you, you must devote all your attention to the baby.
- Figure out how to be a good mom to prove to Earl he didn't make a mistake with you.
- Do not let your baby or Earl down, they are depending on you.

I'm sure most moms can relate to being crazy obsessed with their new babies. I feel this is probably pretty typical, but I have never really known how "normal" moms react to anything. I've had interactions with what I would refer to as "normal" families through my friends and my aunt and uncle. I just never had a true role model to teach me how to be a mom, how to react to situations, how to handle the multitude of raging emotions that flood through your postpartum body. I did not suffer from postpartum depression, so I cannot speak on that topic, except to say it's a real valid issue and if you or someone you know is suffering, please get help.

Most new moms will call their own mom with questions. Everything from changing diapers, babies crying or making weird sounds, and feeding them. Also when you feel like you are doing everything wrong and need to cry or vent to someone, you call your mom so she can tell you everything is going to be okay and you are doing all the right things. I did not have that. While I did have my mother-in-law who was a freakin' saint and I loved her deeply, it still wasn't quite the same.

I was however a VERY determined woman. I was going to create for myself something that I never had. I was going to be the mom that I never had. I was going to build a loving, safe, chaos-free family that I never had. I was going to make our home a safe haven that even after my children were grown, they would want to come back to because they knew it was where love and safety lived. That was my new mission in life. To be that mom. My definition of being a good mom was to put the needs and desires of my child and Earl above all else, including any of my own needs. They would never feel unloved, they would never go without my full attention, they would never feel abandoned or alone.

Journal It Out

- What is the thing you would stand up to a bully for? For me it was my unborn child, it is probably something different for you. This is the thing that puts that fire in your belly. The thought of going without this thing brings on a giant knot of anguish in your pit. It does not have to be something epic. It can be something like quitting smoking, quitting drinking, getting in shape, starting a business, writing a book, becoming a comedian, being a stripper, being vegan, loving animals more than people, civil rights, buying a car, leaving a toxic relationship, getting a haircut, buying a dog….you get the point right? It's whatever is THAT important to you that lights something inside of you, pushing you to do something you may not have done before, stand up for yourself.
- What is more important to you than the person holding you back?

How to break generational trauma.

Steps to help you begin healing the trauma.

Remember to go easy on yourself. This is a process.

1 Self-Awareness. You have to recognize the patterns that you want to change.

2 Courage. Admitting that there are things that need to change will be hard. Be brave.

3 Ownership. Claim what is yours. Stop using an excuse that you do what you do because of others. You can only heal when you own it.

4 Research & Evaluate. Take time to look up what you recognize (addiction, dysfunction, abuse, self-loathing, enabler. Fully understand it and then evaluate how it shows up in your life.

5 Motivation & Support. Stay connected to your goal and find a support system.

6 Patience. Don't expect overnight results, it takes time.

Six

Nuptials

The Proposal

It was June, the baby was sleeping and we were laying on the floor of our living room watching a movie. This was before the days of getting old and getting up off the floor took 47 minutes. My white knight rolled over, looked at me and said, "so you wanna get married or what?" The romance level was off the charts so how could I possibly say no? He is an amazing man, but romance has never been his forte. He did, however, go out that day and get me a ring. Guess he figured he wasn't putting out any money for one unless I said yes.

We were married in August. Yep, two months later. I was not messing around, I wanted to be this man's wife. I was never that little girl who fantasized about her wedding and how special it would be, all the details figured out. I was the girl who fantasized about having a loving family, about having a husband who treated her like a queen, who loved her unconditionally. I fantasized about having kids and loving them like crazy, I wanted to be a mother and a wife. That was my dream. Having a big, fancy wedding was not my thing. There was no chance we were asking anyone to pay for a wedding for us. We lived together and had a baby crying out loud, we were hard core adulting over here, we would pay for our own wedding. Which meant, it had to be very economical. Like I said, I just wanted to be married, the ceremony and reception were just bonuses to share the day with family. I would have been okay with the courthouse. This is how it went down.

We were able to rent a little hall through a family member for $50. We got a family to help "cater" the reception, pot-luck style. We had the mayor of the town marry us at the hall. A friend I worked with made me a bouquet. My grandfather bought a case of wine. We paid for two kegs of beer and two bottles of alcohol for the "pay to dance with the couple and get a shot" tradition. We had a few decorations, nothing fancy. Our biggest expense was a DJ. We shelled out several hundred bucks for 4 hours of music. My aunt bought my dress at Macys. My husband got married in jeans, a button-up shirt, and wrestling shoes. The entire thing was pulled off for probably under $500 and it was perfect. This year, we will be celebrating 23 years married.

My Marriage Lesson for You: Make it about the marriage, not the wedding. Now don't get all offended here that you want the big fancy wedding or that you had the big fancy wedding and I'm telling you not to do that. I'm truly NOT saying don't go balls to the wall and have all the shit your heart desires. If that's your jam, your dream, go for it! Just remember, at the core of the day, it's about the marriage, NOT the wedding. I already had my dream; our wedding was just a celebration of that.

No Change But The Name

After the wedding, not much changed except my last name. I mean, we had already been living together, we had a baby together, what more was there?

Boy, was I mistaken.

How about the added pressure of how to be a good wife? What were the expectations of a wife? Was I supposed to change? I was also now officially a part of his family. How could I make sure that they approved, that I didn't do anything to offend anyone? How was I supposed to integrate myself into this family without upsetting the already perfect balance they had? I mean, we are talking, a full on, healthy family that was so close it was alien to me. How can a family want to spend so much time with each other?

Earl grew up in a very loving family. His parents had been together since high school, he had two older sisters, and they were close. All of them. They actually LIKED spending time with each other.

Shortly after we started dating, his oldest sister met her soulmate. Her and her son moved in with him and began to build their family life together. I was about 7 months pregnant when they got married, it was a very intimate ceremony with just family. They had their first child together about 10 months after I gave birth to our son. A few years later, his middle sister had a baby. Then his oldest sister had her third child, two months later, we had our second. All of the children grew up together, close in ages. We had dinner at his parents' house every single weekend, as a big happy family. We still do to this day, get together once a week. The entire family is still a tight knit group. The kids, while all grown up now, are close. Earl's sisters are our closest friends. We spend as much time as we can with his father, sadly we lost his mother several years ago to cancer.

I share this with you so you can understand what I had married into. This was so out of the norm for me that it was an adjustment getting used to being in a family that liked each other, that spent time together, that was all up in each other's business (in a good way), but still alien to me that people cared so much.

I wanted them to like me. So badly. I had already been in the family for a year and loved them all so much, so really nothing should have changed with getting married. However, for some odd reason, I put added pressure on myself to make sure that I was a perfect wife so that they never doubted my commitment to the family, to their son/brother, to know that he did not make a mistake in picking me.

Defining Expectations

Growing up, I wanted to be a wife and a mother. I never had big aspirations of being the first female President, an astronaut, a successful CEO or a big company or anything fancy like that. The only "career" aspiration I had was to be a fashion designer or something related to fashion because my 13-year-old self thought I was incredibly trendy and was of course going to be the next big thing to hit the runway. My real goal and dream for my life was to be a mother, a really good mom. I wanted to get married, only once. I wanted to have a deep and loving marriage that was a partnership full of respect and kindness and true devotion and passion. I wanted a house full of love and laughter and peace. These were the things I longed for as a kid and what I was determined to make happen when I was an adult.

I would go to friends' houses and it would be calm and quiet. Their parents would be hugging and laughing, they would tuck the kids in at night with a kiss and a smile. It was comforting to know that this type of world existed and I was determined that when I grew up and had a family, this is exactly what my life would be like, happy.

My definition of being a good wife and mother set me up for failure. As with most expectations we put on ourselves, they are filled with grandeur of perfection. They are also incredibly unrealistic and oftentimes lead to utter disappointment and feeling as though we failed miserably.

In my mind, the only way I was going to be viewed as a good wife and mother was to give my husband and children everything they could possibly ever want and even things they didn't think they needed or realized they wanted. Everything that I never had or always thought I wanted is what I was going to give my family. It's important that I point out here that these are NOT things that my husband asked of me, my children did not demand this of me, these are things that I determined was going to make me the absolute best at my job.

Journal It Out

- What is your definition of being a good mom?
- What is your definition of being a good wife?
- What expectations have you put on yourself in motherhood?
- What expectations have you put on yourself in your relationship?
- Do they feel unrealistic or attainable?

Let Go Of Expectations

"Peace is the result of retraining your mind to process life as it is, rahter than how you think it should be." - Wayne Dyer

1 Observe. The expectations you have created have an underlying belief and reason.

2 Awareness. Recognition of the emotions that you experience help you uncover those beliefs.

3 Acceptance. Experience life the way it is. In most instances you have the choice to accept or resist.

4 Practice Gratitude. It is important to be thankful for what you do have. It also empowers you to look for positive outcomes in any situation.

5 Mindfulness. Keeping yourself in the present moment helps you be aware of what you are doing, feeling, and thinking.

Seven

Cutting Ties

Mama Bear

As we continued to settle into our married life as parents, at the young age of 21, we realized, shit is hard. Parenting is exhausting, it's nerve-wracking, it's expensive, and it's terrifying. It's also the best fucking thing I have ever done with my life. I had always wanted to be a mom and achieving that goal did not disappoint. It also made me realize what I wanted in my life and what I didn't. I knew that this family I was creating was the most important thing, that I was going to do whatever it took to keep it safe, I'd wrap it in fucking bubble wrap if I had too, I would protect it. Even if that meant removing toxic relationships from my life that could jeopardize my new family. I was a full-on people-pleasing mama bear not to be messed with.

Ring Ring

Remember how I mentioned that the hubs and I had a very small wedding. That family and friends contributed to the food, pot-luck style? Yep, it was great, like a big ole picnic. My mother and her husband decided they were going to be super-duper generous and buy the deli meats and cheeses for sandwiches.

Side note, they had decided they were getting married that same exact year, only a few months later. And yes, this would be his second wedding and her third, but they needed to go all out, church wedding, big reception, you know. So there was no possible way they could financially contribute anything more to her only daughter's first wedding with anything more than some bologna and ham slices. Alright, fine, whatever, we didn't care, we never asked them for anything anyway, so send over the lunchmeat, it's all good.

The night of our wedding, we had friends from out of town staying at our house and my in-laws took the baby home with them. We got home from the reception, decided we were hungry and headed to a local burger joint. We were having an amazing time. We got back to our house, had a few more drinks, a lot more laughs and then the phone rang. It was probably around 2am at this point. I knew exactly who it was, who else would be calling me this late.

Let me take a moment to explain an aspect of the relationship I had with my mother as an adult. She would get drunk and then call late at night and want to talk, complain, fight, argue, whatever she was into at the moment. Most times it was to start some sort of argument about much of nothing.

"Hello" I answered, knowing damn well it was my drunk ass mother.
    "Where are my meats?" she slurred on the other end.
    Head smack. You have got to be fucking kidding me right. She is calling me at 2am on my wedding night, wanting to know what happened to the lunchmeat she so generously contributed to my wedding reception. You seriously can't make this shit up. We went back and forth for a while about the precious meats and cheeses that she felt should have been left over for her to take home with her.

Now listen, I was part of the clean-up process but had been drinking as well so I can't say for 100% certainty as to whether there were any of the meats and cheeses left, if it got thrown out or if the dumb ass took the leftovers home with her and just didn't remember. (Since this insane 2am drunk phone call, I was advised by other guests that she did in fact, take home all of the luncheon meats and cheeses, that remained). Now that you have some context about the types of late-night phone calls I would receive on the normal, let's get back to that Saturday night before Easter.

When Enough is Enough

It was the Saturday before Easter; I was 24 years old. This was the day I decided to cut my mother out of my life. It was not what I thought the day would bring when I got out of bed that morning, but life is full of surprises. As with any holiday, we had already decided on the details of how we would split our time between our families. We had originally decided we would go to my mother's first and then we would end the day with Earl's family.

Another drunk call came in, she was wanting to fight about how we always spend more time with my husband's family. I have to admit, I don't remember exactly what we were fighting about that night aside from where we were spending the majority of our holiday time. I am certain there were some nasty things said, definitely some slurring and me hitting my breaking point. While this was not the last time I spoke to my mother, this was the moment that I decided that my family was going to take priority over trying to please her and to keep her and the toxicity that her and husband #3 brought into my life. I was an adult and I held the power to decide how I let others treat me and I was done allowing this bullshit to continue, it was not going to impact my marriage and it damn well wasn't going to infect my son. Put a fork in me, I was done.

We did not go to their house the next day. We have not been to their house since. My son, who is now 23, has not seen her since he was 3 years old. My daughter, who is 18, has never met her. While this hasn't always been an easy decision to hold onto, it was the best decision for me, my mental health, and my family.

I have received phone calls several times since that night. A few weeks after our last big fight and my decision to be done, we received a message on our answering machine. Yes, this was a long time ago back when physical answering machines attached to landline phones were a thing. We got home one day and there was that blinking red light demanding attention.

We hit the button and a woman's voice came across thanking my husband for the fun time last night and how she can't wait to do it again. I make eye contact with my husband and after a few minutes we both just start laughing. Why the hell would I be laughing at the mention of my husband being with another woman? First of all, I immediately recognized the voice as a friend of my mothers. Second, my husband and I were together the entire day and night the previous day. This was just some of the shenanigans they tried to pull to break us up. Jokes on them, we have now been married for almost 23 years.

I share this with you because this is an example of what they did to us after we cut them out of our lives. They were determined to make me lose my baby when they found out I was pregnant and they were determined to cause problems in my marriage when I finally stood up for myself. These are not the actions of loving and supportive parents and provide some of the reasoning as to why I am no longer associated with them nor have not allowed them to be in the lives of my children.

Making decisions to change your life is not always easy. Taking the steps to remove toxic people from your life is incredibly painful, stressful, and a difficult thing to do. However, if these people do more harm than good and have zero fucking intention of ever changing that, don't you think you deserve the right to decide if you want to be a part of that? And if you make the decision for yourself, your family, and your wellbeing that there is no place in your future for them, give yourself permission to cut those ties.

It's not always going to be easy. There have been more times than I can count that I want so badly to have my mother in my life. So many times I wished things could be different. All of the times that I want to reach out, that I think about calling, that I have a glimmer of hope that I could have loving parents in my life are countered with the reality. What I really crave from my parents is something they can never give me. I have moments where I fantasize about what if but that's all it is. A fantasy of what ifs. I have an idea of what it could be like in my heart, but in my logical mind I know that I will never get what I want from them and if I was to open the door to let them back in, it would just lead to more chaos and more heartbreak. That is not something I am willing to risk putting myself or my family through. So as hard as the decision has been, it is one that I stand behind. Because that is our right as women, as mothers, as humans, to have enough love for ourselves to make tough decisions and stand with the outcome.

They Are Called Boundaries

According to Wikipedia, personal boundaries are guidelines, rules or limits that a person creates to identify reasonable, safe, and permissible ways for other people to behave towards them and how they will respond when someone passes those limits.

Interesting concept, but what the fuck did that really even mean and how exactly are you supposed to set said boundaries, or determine what they should be? I did not grow up in a world where we learned how to create healthy boundaries for ourselves, how to ensure that we kept our own energy protected, that we could say no when it was not truly beneficial to ourselves and those around us. We did not learn appropriate response tools when we were upset or angry or felt attacked. Hence, the people-pleasing. That was my coping mechanism.

I don't have rules and limits for how other people are "allowed" to behave towards me. I have rules and limits on how I lock shit up nice and tight in the vault in the pit of my stomach and I make sure that others personal boundaries are at the forefront. That what they need, what they allow, their rules and limits are achieved.

Setting a personal boundary was giving myself permission to accept that I have needs that deserve to be met. It was admitting that saying "no" to someone was acceptable and not going to start an apocalypse.

The first boundary I set was keeping my baby safe. That was an absolute line in the sand that was not crossed. My baby was going to be kept safe no matter what, no matter who thought otherwise. The second boundary I set was keeping my family safe. I was not going to let outside influences have any impact on my family bubble. It would always feel loved and protected by me. When it came time to set a boundary that was just about me, that was harder. The first two still met my people-pleasing addiction because they involved my child and my husband. I wasn't ready to go head first into setting boundaries that were all about me, it's okay to take it slow. Baby steps my friends.

Journal It Out

- Can you think of a time in your life when you set a boundary?
- How about a time when you felt you should have set one but just couldn't do it?
- Why was setting it hard for you?
- Where are some other areas you wish had better boundaries?

- What is one simple thing you can do to set that boundary?

Setting Boundaries.

A boundary is a limit you set for yourself that will determine what you will or will not participate in.

1 Name your limits. Consider what you can handle and where you get stressed/uncomfortable

2 Be direct. You may have to be assertive in sticking up for yourself, especially first. Use a clear and direct dialogue.

3 Give yourself permission. Release the guilt. Remember, boundaries are a sign of self-respect.

4 Self-Awareness. Tune into your feelings. Safeguard your space.

5 Learn to say "no", this one will be hard. Practice. Start small.

6 Self-Care is a must. Ask for what you want. It's OK to put yourself first.

Eight

Martyrdom

Same Only Different

You would think that setting all of these boundaries with my toxic family would have been all I needed to do, right? Life isn't as simple as that though. My trauma response of people-pleasing didn't end when those relationships did, it continued on into my new family, but it looked a lot different.

When we decided we wanted baby #2, it took a lot longer than getting pregnant the first time. We tried for over a year before seeing a doctor about why it was taking so long. I had been diagnosed with PCOS and endometriosis which was adding to the difficulty of conceiving. After about a year and a half, we finally got the joyous news, we were pregnant. That was just the start of all the times my faith would be tested, the entire pregnancy was filled with trials and tribulations. Initially our doctor thought it was an ectopic pregnancy, which thankfully was not the case. For the next 8 ½ months, I went to appointments and tests non-stop. We were told multiple times that there would be things wrong with our girl. At one point, they wanted to do a test where they would stick a big ass needle in my stomach to see what sort of "disabilities" she would have and that would allow us to decide if we wanted to proceed with the pregnancy.

For us, there was no question that no matter what, we were moving forward with having this baby, which meant I did not feel the test was needed and declined. At 6 months pregnant, I was put on bed rest. Pretty tough to do when you have a 5-year-old running around! After almost 3 long months of laying around, doing more than I should and getting yelled at constantly by everyone, it was time! When she blessed us with her presence, she was perfect. Darian Elizabeth entered the world as a tiny, healthy little peanut. At first, the doctor had a concern that she might have a small hole at the base of her spine, but after more testing, it turned out to be nothing. She had finally arrived and she was everything we could have imagined we wanted or needed to complete our family.

After such a stressful and trying pregnancy, I decided two kids is where we would stop. We had always talked about wanting 3 children, but why test fate. We had two beautiful and healthy children; we were complete. To be completely honest, I did not think I could mentally or physically go through another pregnancy like that.

We settled into being a family of four and after 3 months of maternity leave, it was time to head back to work. I was a full-time working mom up until Darian was 10 months old. This would have been around 2003 that I quit my job and became a stay-at-home mom. She got sick. It was scary as fuck. Here's the story.

A Trip To Children's Hospital

My husband was working the night shift, I was home with the kids, trying to get everyone to sleep because I had to work in the morning. My daughter who, as mentioned above, was about 10 months old, had not been feeling well, she was very fussy and didn't want to sleep. My son was tucked in and snoozing while I was in the living room with the baby trying to get her to sleep, praying to the heavens above for the strength to continue pacing the floor with a screaming baby. I put a blanket on the floor and laid her down to change her. As I was looking at her, she looked like she was having trouble breathing, then her chest started to cave in. Seriously. Her chest was actually caving in as she was trying so hard to get a breath, but just couldn't. Well, of course, I immediately went into a full-on fucking panic. I had no idea what to do, so I called the pediatrician who immediately made my panic skyrocket by telling me I needed to get her to the ER ASAP. WTF.

Tears immediately begin falling down my face as I try to hold my shit together long enough to come up with a plan. This was before the entire world had a cell phone, so I had no way of getting in touch with my husband because calling him at work was not an option either. I called my in-laws to explain what was happening and to meet me at the hospital to get my son. I wrote a note to tell my husband what was going on and left it on the table. I wrapped everyone up and headed out. We lived maybe 7 minutes from the hospital, but damn it was a long fucking drive. We got to the ER and I got her checked in and then we waited. My in-laws showed up shortly after that, we talked briefly and they took my son with them so that he could get some sleep and not have to sit in a hospital room all night.

When we were finally called back into the Emergency Department, they began hooking her up to IVs and giving her breathing treatments. After several hours at the hospital, our pediatrician decided that we needed to go to Children's Hospital, by ambulance. I used the hospital phone to call my husband and let him know what was going on, by this time, he would have arrived at home and hopefully found the note. I filled him in and we made a plan that I would ride in the ambulance and he would meet me there. He would take care of calling his parents to let them know we needed them to keep our son while we were with our daughter.

Going through the entire ordeal of the ambulance ride, checking in at the new hospital, trying to find my husband, scared out of my mind and not having a mental breakdown was exhausting. They were trying to give her a breathing treatment and she was screaming, I was bawling my eyes out, and Earl was trying to comfort me. It was a train wreck. After that, they put her in the NICU and that is where we remained for 3 days. After two days, my two aunts, Sherry and Jo, came down to check on us. They agreed to sit with my baby girl while we went home to shower and for me to get some supplies to stay at the hospital. My husband had just started a new job a few weeks prior to this happening, so he was not able to take time away. We agreed that I would stay at the hospital, our son would remain with my in-laws and he would be at the hospital every minute he wasn't working. At this point, we had no idea how long we would be there.

After the first night, when my husband and I slept beside her crib in the NICU, they decided we could no longer do this. Children's Hospital provides rooms for parents to stay in when your child is there long term. I had no idea if we were going to be long-term and there were currently no rooms available, so I slept in waiting rooms. I used my purse as a pillow because I was afraid it would be stolen (yes I know, paranoid) and my coat as a blanket. I didn't think I'd actually be able to get any sleep this way, but I was so exhausted, mentally and physically that I think my body just shut down. I don't know how much "rest" I actually got because when I woke up, I still felt drained. I mean, it's not like I was at the Ritz Carlton in a plush bed, I was sleeping on a rock hard two-person chair in a hospital waiting room.

On day 4, when I woke up and went to see my girl, she wasn't there. You want to talk about a fucking panic attack, I lost my shit. They had moved her overnight and didn't tell me. I was freaking the fuck out, on everyone around me. Not cool, I know, but my baby was gone and nobody told me, even though I specifically told them where to find me if ANYTHING happened. We stepped down from the NICU, she had stabilized enough that she no longer needed constant watch, this was amazing news. After a full day and night here (can't remember what this department was called), we were sent to an actual room. We spent two nights in this room and we were finally discharged. Hallelujah, we got to go home!

While I was thrilled to leave the hospital, they never were able to determine what caused her breathing issues. She would need to receive breathing treatments multiple times per day to prevent a relapse until they could figure out the root of the problem. This was a lot to put on my father in law who was our babysitter at the time, so we made the decision for me to quit working and stay home and take care of her.

This was just one of the bumps in the road where I felt I could carry the weight of it all alone. I needed to take as much of the pain and burden as I could to make sure that my husband and children were alright. I continued this path for years to come, we faced countless struggles that tested us as individuals, as a couple, as parents. Those struggles became much easier once I realized I didn't have to go through them as a people-pleaser and allowed myself to go through them as a person, a wife, a mother and lean on the family around me to help me.

The Family Martyr

A martyr often refers to a person who unnecessarily sacrifices themselves for others, while ignoring their own needs. I gave up everything else about my life except for my kids and my husband. I let go of friends, hobbies, self-care, even my job. Not that my job was something I wanted to hold onto, just getting my point across. I never had a career, I've always just had jobs to pay the bills, giving it up to be a stay-at-home mom was a blessing. At which point, I threw everything I had into being the best mother and wife I could be. In my mind, the fact that I didn't work outside of the home any longer meant that my husband shouldn't have to do a single thing aside from getting up, going to work, then coming home and allowing me to do everything for him. Yes, seriously, this is what I thought it should be.

My children did not have chores, my husband did not need to help around the house, it was my job to take care of everything for them. If I'm being honest, if they did do something, I usually went back and did it again anyway. I took care of all the housework inside and out. I did ask my kids to clean up their rooms or pick up after themselves, but it was not an issue I pushed. I did all the cleaning, laundry, cooking, and running kids to all their errands. I was the receptionist/secretary for the family. I mowed the grass, trimmed the hedges, took care of the animals, did the banking, paid the bills, and went shopping. I did almost everything (my choice).

The only thing that I did not take care of was vehicle maintenance. I pretty much made myself into a servant to make sure that they were taken care of in the best way I knew how. They would sit on the couch watching TV or playing games and ask for a drink so I'd run and get it for them. This is how I felt I needed to serve my family to show them how much I loved them, I wanted more than anything else to be the best mom and wife and this is how I felt I did it. *People-pleasing much?*

I mean, I was never treated this way so that meant that doing this was how you showed love. Serving them, waiting on them hand and foot was how they would know that they were loved and cherished right? If they were required to get their own drink or pack their own lunch, they might get mad or upset. What kind of mother would I be if my kids were always mad at me? I don't want my husband to be upset because I ask him for help around the house, he works all day, he doesn't deserve to be treated that way. No, everyone will be much happier, calmer, and at ease if I just do everything for everyone.

People-Pleaser Burnout

I know, so many of you reading this either think I'm crazy or you can relate. Either way, it's cool. This was the life I created, it wasn't meant for anyone else to mimic or judge, it was my way. I'm sure you can imagine that years of this can burn a person out. However, when you are a people-pleaser, you don't acknowledge your own issues! You just put your head down and push through while trying to hide any true emotions or feelings you're experiencing. That's what I did. I felt I was doing a pretty bang-up job of it. There was no way that my family had any clue that I was suffering or in pain. I didn't miss a moment of tending to their every need. My kids didn't miss school or practices or games. My husband was always woken up for work with breakfast ready, lunch packed, and dinner ready when he got home.

When you live this life, you don't take care of yourself. Like ever. That would be selfish and you would feel no pleasure, nothing but guilt. I did not take time for myself; I did not have friends; I did everything with my family or for my family.

When you spend your entire life putting the needs of everyone else above yourself, it's easy to get lost. I spent my entire childhood lost, looking for love and validation. My teen years were a blur of trying to fit in, not wanting to stand out, looking for acceptance. My late teen, early adult years were me searching for something, trying to find myself, I guess. I went into motherhood and marriage with the same philosophy that I used growing up - if you please everyone around you, don't talk about what you want or need, life will be easier.

The problem was all the years of putting everyone else first and no regard for yourself will eventually catch up to you. There will come a time when all of the pain and trauma you have shoved deep down and ignored will bubble to the surface. At some point in your journey, you are going to have to confront your demons. That time in my life was coming. It was like the hot lava of a volcano bubbling under the surface ready to burst. Shit was about to get explosive.

Journal It Out

- Where in your life are you playing the martyr? This isn't limited to motherhood like my story, you could also be doing this in your relationships, your career, etc.
- Try setting a boundary using what you learned in the last chapter to help you begin to bring awareness to your martyrdom and one step you can take towards releasing that title.

Recognizing patterns of a martyr.

The destructive behavior in which a person habitually seeks suffering or persecution as a way to feel "good" about themselves.

1 Exhibit signs of low self-esteem or confidence.

2 Come from a background of abuse. Emotionally or physically.

3 Exagerate levels of suffering or sacrafice to make themselves look better.

4 When a problem get solved, actively seeking out another problem to solve or complain about.

5 Inability to accept responsibility for actions that have caused pain or suffering.

6 Inability to set boundaries and say "no"

Resources From Chapter 1

I felt it was important to share them again here. Remember, asking for help is a sign of strength, not weakness. If you recognize you are at a breaking point and unsure what to do, here are some resources for you to turn to. Ask for my help my friend. (*I know it's a scary thought but* **TRUST** *me, it's okay and* **YOU** *deserve to receive the help you need*).

- National Suicide Prevention Lifeline, 1-800-273-8255; you can also text HELLO to 741741. Both services are available 24/7.
- Veterans Crisis Line, 1-800-273-8255 & press 1; text 838255; chat via veteranscrisisline.net All services available 24/7 for service members and their families.
- Domestic Violence 800.799.SAFE (7233), TheHotline.org (chat option available); Available 24/7, Confidential
- BetterHelp (Online Counseling App)
- TalkLife (Mental Health Support App)
- Teladoc (App, website, or call 800-teladoc)
- Reach out to a Religious Leader you trust
- Call a family member or friend
- Check with your employer for any EAP resources (Employee Assistance Programs), lots of employers provide them and they offer mental health resources, therapy, etc.

Nine

Tick Tick Boom

⚜

Being An Ass

From a very young age I used people pleasing to protect myself. It was my trauma response. It kept me safe in a situation no child should ever be put into. It served me so well that I survived and got out. The only problem was that "the one, or so I thought" broke my heart and caused even more people pleasing wounds. People pleasing became the thing that I used in my marriage and in my new family with my children to keep everyone happy. This is what I had used for so long and had worked for so long to keep me safe and finally loved. I didn't want to let anyone down and I didn't want to be left or to go back to what my life used to be like.

This is how I ended up lost in motherhood and marriage. The fact that all I ever wanted my entire life was to have a family, you would think I would have been on top of the world happy that my dream became my reality. Don't get me wrong, I was happy in the general sense of the term, I was beyond grateful for my kids and my husband. I have two healthy kids that are decent human beings and I have a husband who is an incredible dad, husband, and person. And he loves me unconditionally. Yet, even given all of that, I was miserable.

As a mom, we go through what our children go through. When they hurt, we hurt. When they feel joy and happiness, so do we. As a people-pleaser and an empath, I carried it all deep inside me, I did not share it. I felt it was my job to hold onto any of the pain or stress and try to alleviate them from it. After so many years of doing this, I finally hit a wall. I was depressed, had anxiety daily, and suffered from panic attacks. All while trying to hide it from everyone and keep trucking along like I always did, thinking I would be FINE. I wasn't fine. I was suffering in silence. Remember Chapter 1? We are back at that point in the story. I felt like I needed to carry EVERYTHING for EVERYONE around me. I did not want my husband or my children to experience anything but calm happiness. I was a fucking donkey, in a few ways! I was trying to haul around the burdens of everyone, including my own. I was also being an ass thinking it was okay to put that kind of stress on myself. My husband and children didn't ask this of me, I put all the pressure on myself and then I crumbled underneath the weight.

The Final Straw

As the kids were getting older and needed me less, I had more time myself. Which should have been an amazing thing, what most parents wait for. Time for themselves, time for their marriage. For me however, I had no idea what the fuck to do with all of this time. This was giving my brain too many opportunities for my thoughts to run rampant. Those thoughts were ugly bitches and they were taking over. I already shared many of the nasty things being said to me by the bitch living inside my brain in Chapter 1 so I won't bore you with those details again.

The basic gist of it was this. I did not have any respect or love for myself. I did not feel I provided any value to my family any longer. I felt alone. I felt sad. Just sad all the time, I can't really explain it otherwise. Suicidal thoughts were happening pretty regularly and yes, they scared the shit out of me, but as we know, I was too much of a people-pleaser to act on them. While I came close a few times, the thoughts of what it would do to my husband and kids always prevented me from following through with it. That's what I always told myself until the day I was trying to find an insurance policy that still paid out even in the event of suicide. When I was sitting at the computer googling how to kill myself to look like an accident. Those two instances made me realize how serious it was. Even if I never followed through with my whack ass suicide thoughts, did I really want to live this way?

I had panic attacks almost daily at work. I would curl myself into a fetal position on the floor of my office and sob. I could be doing the most mundane task of washing dishes or folding laundry and I would just start crying. It was hard to find joy in my days. When just getting out of bed in the mornings takes every ounce of energy you have, actually enjoying your day or any aspect of it would take a miracle and that is exactly what I prayed for.

I had two amazing kids. I had a husband who loved me. We had built this beautiful life together, but I was too deep in my state of depression to appreciate what I had. I did not want to continue to wake up every day and force myself to live my life.

Leap Of Faith

When I asked for help, it was the hardest thing I have ever done. And I gave birth twice without medication! I want you to listen to me very carefully here. When you say that you don't think you can ask for help or you don't know how to ask for help, I understand where you are coming from, truly I do. Let me just run a scenario for you to consider.

Imagine if you will, you wake up in the morning, feeling refreshed and energized. You are ready to start your morning routine because you actually want to, not because you have too. You spend time with your spouse and kids, you are laughing and truly enjoying yourself. You find joy and happiness in all the little mundane things you do to keep your family running. You are not suffering from all of the physical ailments that depression puts on you, but rather you are full of energy and LIFE! You are living your life and you are loving every second of it.

THIS can be your reality. It is completely up to you to make it happen. It's a choice. You need to take a leap of faith, reach out for help, ask for support, and when it is offered, you take it. There is no going back, only moving forward. You are worth it. I know it might not feel like it right now but that is why you are reaching out for help.

From The Darkness

When I first started getting help, it came from a program at my job. My employer offered a program called EAP (employee assistance program) that provided you with free therapy sessions. I utilized those 8 free sessions then I spoke to a doctor (within the same practice) regarding getting some medication to help regulate all the shit going on in my brain.

A note about therapists, if you don't like the one you are with, that is not an excuse to give up and walk away. It is a reason to look for a new one. I have had 4 therapists over the years. It's important to find someone that you jive with, someone you are comfortable with, someone you can open up with and look forward to seeing, not just another item on your to-do list. If your first one doesn't fit, keep looking!

It hasn't always been easy working with a therapist. My first few sessions were incredibly awkward. I didn't know what to say, I had no idea what to share or what I wanted them to know or what I wanted to keep to myself. I did not understand why I was suffering from depression and anxiety so I did not know the first way to begin to work through it. After a few sessions, it got a little easier. The therapist was able to guide me with questions and prompt me to open up. It just continued to get easier from there and even more so when I truly found a therapist I clicked with. She is an absolute life-saver for me, a partner in my mental wellbeing and I have no qualms in telling her everything that I am dealing with, everything that I am feeling. It is a judgement free zone and that is a freeing experience.

After some time working with a therapist, it was easier to admit what I had been going through to family and let them know that I needed support. This was not something I was able to admit immediately, I had to get over the initial shame I carried around it before I could be honest with those closest to me. There is so much taboo surrounding mental health and that causes those of us who suffer to do so in silence, to try and hide it, to carry guilt and shame around it. Overcoming that is not easy and it will look different for everyone. For me, it didn't happen right away. I was on my medication and working with a therapist for about two months before I was able to openly talk about what I was experiencing with anyone. And even those initial conversations with those who loved me unconditionally, I held back.

I did not share the extent of my suffering until probably a year after I started my healing. It is also important for me to mention that how someone else reacts to what you are going through has nothing to do with you. My husband did not have a great reaction to my confession of depression and suicidal thoughts (understandably) and my gut response was to comfort him and "people-please" him through the emotions that it brought up for him. However, that was and still is not my job when anything tough comes up. It was my responsibility to share my story with him, it's his responsibility to work through the feelings it brings up for him. It is also not his responsibility to "fix me." It's his responsibility to be there for me and to support me on my healing path.

If you are feeling shame around your own situation, I'd like to tell you to knock that shit off and forget about the bullshit stigma that has been shackled to mental health, but I know that you have to get there on your own, you have to work through it on your own, even though I would like you to listen to me since I've already been there. I know it's a road that you have to travel and navigate on your own, nobody can tell you how to do it. It's been over 2 years and I still see a therapist regularly. There is no longer shame around it because it helps me and that makes it worth it to me. Regardless of what anyone thinks.

Journal It Out

- Are you ready to ask for help? Who can you talk to that is close to you? A spouse, a friend, a parent, another family member, your clergy, a colleague, your HR dept at work. If you feel alone and that you do not have anyone to turn to please use the resources section and find someone to reach out too.

- Check in with your emotions, are you always feeling sad, angry, resentful, betrayed, unappreciated, unseen, unloved, anxious, worried, afraid, alone?

- Check in with your body, what are the physical symptoms that you are experiencing?

- What do you wish you could experience and feel in your body day to day instead?

- Get honest with yourself and write down how you feel. I mean TRULY feel, your emotions, what you go through on a regular basis, you deep down thoughts and feelings. It's important to be honest with yourself. None of the sugar-coating bullshit here. It is ok to put that brave face on for others but this is where we are getting real, getting serious, getting vulnerable. If you can't get honest with yourself, you will not be willing to take the step towards help. And remember this, what you write is for you. It's not for anyone else. If you fear someone seeing what you write, when you are done destroy it. Burn it, rip it up, throw it in the ocean, whatever works for you, just get your thoughts on paper, open up, be real.

How to ask for help.

Tips to guide you to support so you can begin to heal and grow. .

1 Determine what you need. Only you know what that is,

2 Do not apologize when asking for the help.

3 Be specific. Let people know what you ACTUALLY need and BE HONEST.

4 Do not assume you know how someone will react or what their response will be to you.

5 Do it when you feel comfortable, let go of the stigma you have built up around it, then ask.

6 Asking for help is not a sign of weakness, it takes great courage to admit when you need help so do not let that stigma stop you.

Ten

Turning Points

~⁂~

Healing The Trauma

My healing journey began when I started receiving help after I had finally hit rock bottom. It started with prescription medication from my doctor for depression and anxiety. Then came the licensed therapists, whom I still see to this day and don't have any intention of giving up anytime soon. After almost a year of therapy and medication, I was finally feeling like myself again. It was not exactly an easy year to get through, I will not pretend that asking for help and actually accepting it, was not without challenges. And I also will not pretend that just because I accepted the help, was receiving said help, that it is a one and done sort of situation. That I never had to argue with myself to continue accepting the help that people were giving, that I didn't have to talk myself into feeling I deserved it.

I still have days like that and it's important to understand that if you also have days like that, don't be hard on yourself, it's okay. It is an unrealistic expectation to put on yourself to think you can be sunshine and rainbows every fucking day. You are setting yourself up for failure if you do. We are human beings with a treasure trove of emotions, we have to allow ourselves to feel them all, sit with them, have bad days, have good days. You know the saying, take the good with the bad, it's like that. In order to have the sunshine and rainbows, you have to also have the dark clouds and thunderstorms.

To be honest, I had no idea that most of my issues stemmed from my childhood. Crazy right? To an outsider looking in or me looking back now, it's logical to see how the shit that happened during my childhood fucked me up, but I couldn't really see it until I started to get some real help, until I started to dig deep and do some inner work and healing. I am also pointing this out because when you are inside of the situation, it is normal. Sure, I saw other kid's childhoods, but to me my experience was normal.

After about a year of getting all of this help, I started to seek out more on my own. I knew that something was missing, that I wanted something more, that I desired a deeper level of healing, and that I wanted more inner peace. I just didn't know how or where to find it. I also knew that I wanted to find some holistic approaches to treating my depression and anxiety beyond medication because to be honest, I suck with meds. No, seriously, I'm terrible at taking them consistently and for whatever reason, I just hate taking medicine.

Let's Get Physical

I have suffered from headaches and migraines for years. When I would mention it to my doctor, he would offer up a medication I could take to help. Well, as I mentioned above, I suck at meds and honestly, I didn't want to have to just keep medicating the symptoms, I wanted someone to tell me the REASON I had these chronic pains.

One day, I was in a therapy session, I was non-stop yawning and constantly rubbing my neck and temples. She asked me if I was okay. I shrugged my shoulders and just started crying for no good reason. Exhaustion maybe, I don't know, but I couldn't stop the tears from streaming down. Through my sobs and snot, I tried explaining how exhausted I was, how I have a headache every single day, that my stomach constantly feels like it's in knots. I'm so restless and can't seem to just sit still. I drive myself crazy wringing my hands, crunching my toes or moving my feet in circles. Isn't it enough that I am sad ALL THE TIME, do I have to also have all these other odd fucking glitches?

She handed me a box of kleenex and told me to take a deep breath. She explained that when you are suffering from depression, anxiety, and panic attacks you will probably encounter what I was dealing with. She reminded me that it's important for people to understand that physical symptoms can manifest from mental illness. This was such a relief for me to understand that one, I wasn't alone in how I was feeling and two, I wasn't going crazy and these physical symptoms weren't just in my head.

An Alternative Comfort Zone

I started looking into some holistic alternatives for not only dealing with the anxiety and depression, but also to help with the physical symptoms. This searching led me to discover all sorts of possible alternatives, options that I had no idea even existed! Things like journaling, meditation, massages, spirituality, books, podcasts, Reiki, prayer, yoga, acupuncture, and essential oils.

Most of these practices felt out of my comfort zone and too far outside my capacity at the time. I needed tangible and easy things I could incorporate into a day that was already overwhelming. I could not imagine adding ALL THE THINGS, it was just too much. As I read about all these different modalities that were all the rage on the internet, I knew I needed to pick one or two things that felt achievable. The idea that there were so many options available to help me when I was ready for them was comforting.

Listening to a podcast felt easy, it felt achievable. I was lying in bed and opened up the Podcast app on my iPhone. I searched for Joel Osteen. I am a fan of his and when I catch his shows on TV they always make me feel better so I figured it was a great place to start. I subscribed to his Podcast and hit play on an episode called *Recognizing Your Value.* It talked about learning to see your value not from other people or things, but from within, from who God made you to be. It was enough encouragement for me to get out of bed and shower, to actually start my day. I started listening to podcasts almost daily, as a source of inspiration. It was easy to put one on and listen while I was lying in bed or getting a shower. Once I started to feel comfortable with adding that into my day, I was ready to build on that and add something else.

This is when I decided to journal. My therapist is also a fan of journaling and encouraged using it to help me work through some of the pain and trauma. I bought a journal at Michaels and spent a few minutes each day writing down how I was feeling or what was going on that day. It took a while, probably weeks or even a month or two to start seeing any results, but it is my number one recommendation to anyone who is suffering or struggling. There is something about the connection of putting your thoughts to paper that is a form of release, it's very therapeutic. Remember that there is no wrong way to journal, just let yourself write, release your feelings and emotions and see what comes up.

Another resource for me was books, *oh so many books.* I started my own fucking library of personal development books, seriously I became a bit of a hoarder! I devoured anything that could help me heal from my past and grow towards my future. I continue to use this trio of modalities to help me to heal my trauma and treat my mental health.

I Have An Oil For That

I heard on a Podcast one day about using Lavender Essential Oil. The claim was that it was a miracle fix for relaxing, sleeping, helping anxiety, and so much more. I was pretty hesitant, but decided to give it a try anyway. I pulled up the Amazon app and did a quick search for "lavender essential oils." I was flooded with options, so many that I didn't have any idea what to pick! I started reading reviews until I found one that sounded promising, along with a diffuser. Add to cart, checkout, wait 2 days, thank you Prime. When it arrived, I was anxious to give it a try. I opened up the lavender, took a big inhale in and waited for the magic to happen. As you can imagine, no birds started to sing, no rainbow shot out my ass, it was just me standing there holding a bottle and sniffing it waiting for something to happen, looking slightly ridiculous, I'm sure.

I set up the diffuser in my bedroom, added drops of the oil, turned it on, laid down on my bed and waited. After about 15 minutes, I gave up and left the room. A few hours later, it was time to go to sleep. I figured it was another sleepless night ahead of me, but surprisingly, that night, I slept more soundly than I had in months. A fluke I thought. I continued the same ritual every night for a week. I also noticed when I diffused the oil during the day, my anxiety didn't run as rampant. It was still there, but I had days where it didn't seem to run my entire day. There just might be some magic to these oils after all.

I decided I wanted to learn more about the use of essential oils, so much so that I ended up studying and becoming a certified aromatherapist. This was the first time I decided to do something for me and because I alone wanted to do it. This was a huge shift from only doing things to meet the needs of and keep my family happy.

I began to use essential oils daily, I would diffuse them in my office while working to help with my anxiety. I diffused them in my bedroom at night to promote rest and comfort. I created blends for my meditation practice. I have personal inhalers that contain blends that work for me when I feel anxious or depressed. Using essential oils is part of my wellness ritual. I use them in all aspects of my home and life, integrating them into my self-care. Be sure to check out the resources section for some of my favorite diffuser blends.

Meeting My Gremlin

I mentioned that as part of my holistic wellness path, podcasts became a daily resource. I started researching for ones that provided inspiration, spirituality, mindset, growth, all of the personal development keywords. I came across The Badass Manifester Podcast which focused on manifestation. That is how I found Ashley Gordon. She is the creator of the Badass Manifester Podcast and of The Quantum Coach Brand. She is an absolutely beautiful human being; she is a powerhouse coach and business woman. She also happened to write the incredible forward for this book! She was my first business coach; she is my mentor and she will forever be my friend.

She created a digital program called "Create Your Life On Purpose." I remember her talking about it on one of the podcasts and immediately thought, I need this. This was the next step on my journey, it was time to start figuring out what was next. Signing up for the program was such a pivotal moment for me, it was the first time I decided to invest in myself in what I considered an out of the box expense. Meaning it wasn't just for my meds or therapy or a book. This was something completely new and different for me and taking that leap was scary. When we go outside of our normal, it can be terrifying, but it is the perfect opportunity for expansion and growth. Nothing changes if nothing changes. To really heal and shift the trajectory of my life's direction, I needed to leave my comfort zone. That is what making an investment into this course was for me, a leap of faith that I deserved to have the chance at the life I desired.

One of the most pivotal shifts I experienced during the course was using an exercise Ashley refers to as the "GAIL" method. (With her permission,

I'm going to share a glimpse into this method which you can locate in the *Resources Section*.) This method has to do with recognizing the voice in your head that tells you all the negative shit and limiting beliefs that hold you back. It helps you get to the root of where that voice comes from and work through the beliefs that may not actually be your true core beliefs, your values, your actual truth. It allows you to really look at the filter and the judgement that you place on yourself and your life. It was my first introduction into limiting beliefs and how to start working through them. It helped me to see that the bitch in my head was put there not by me, but by all of the things I was told or learned through childhood.

I grew up what we will refer to as financially challenged. Like standing in the free food line at the church, probably can't pay the electric bill this month, challenged. I can remember wanting to get a pair of Jordache Jeans (yes it was the 80's), this adorable pair of acid-washed jeans with zippers at the back hem with a bow at the top of the zipper. These jeans were LIFE and I needed them! My friends all had cool jeans like this, I was certain that to continue being in that friend group, I would absolutely need these jeans. I was terrified to ever ask for anything specific that I wanted, I did not want to upset the balance of calm, but these jeans were that important, I was willing to rock the boat at the chance of making them mine!

The day I worked up the nerve to ask my mom for them, she snickered at me and said "Do you think money grows on trees? I work hard for my money not to be wasted on a stupid pair of jeans." What does this have to do with my gremlin you ask? This 60 second interaction sent a message to my unconscious mind that what I want is frivolous and stupid, money is hard to come by, you have to work hard for money and make sure you don't waste it. I have carried these beliefs with me since that day. That is how limiting beliefs work, they are the "gremlin." One tiny moment, that may seem insignificant at the time, can plant a rock-solid belief in your brain that can determine how you live your life, the choices you make, and the actions you take or don't take.

As I started to re-wire what I actually believed, I was able to shift my thought process to understand I actually deserve peace and happiness. I deserve to ask for and receive what I want. It helped me begin to let go of the self-doubt that consumed me and to start building up my self-worth.

Another thing I discovered when working through my limiting beliefs and confronting my gremlin was that I was angry. I held tons of resentment in my heart. I was angry and resentful at my parents for not being who I wanted or needed them to be. I was angry and resentful of myself for all of the mistakes and poor choices I had made over my life. When you go through your life filled with hurt, anger, and sadness, you take away space for joy, laughter, and love.

I needed to forgive. Everyone and everything that I was letting take up valuable space in my heart and soul needed to be forgiven and released. I realized how deeply it was holding me back. I lived in the past. I blamed so much on my upbringing, my parents, my bad decisions. I let it all be a crutch, an excuse to stay small, to not live the big life I wanted and desired. All of the negative, all of the bad, all of the pain and hurt was my permission slip to continue to fuck up, to continue to make bad decisions, to just "get by" in my every day instead of "living" in my every day.

The F Word

Forgiveness. It's a doozy. It's a hype word in the world of internet self-help which can make it sound like an easy thing. Just forgive and move on. Bitch please, if it's that easy, are you really, truly forgiving and healing? I guess it's truly dependent upon you. How easily are you able to forgive someone, heal from the situation, and move on. It's not up to me or the internet to determine that for you. Only you know within yourself what it's going to take for you to provide the forgiveness required to release yourself from the pain, the hurt, the trauma, and your attachment to the situation.

The real question for you at this point is do you feel you deserve to move past it? Do you feel that forgiveness should or could be given? Is the thought of it too overwhelming for you? If it is, then I would say you have more work to do within yourself before you can begin this practice. Forgiving someone or forgiving yourself is not the first step in a healing journey. You have to get yourself ready for a shift of that proportion.

When I walked into my first therapy appointment all those years ago, if my therapist would have said, "okay it's now time to forgive yourself and your parents" I would have told her to fuck off and walked out. Even on the day that my coach talked to me about forgiveness, I gave a big ole eye roll thinking no fucking way this is going to work, keep in mind this day came years after my healing journey began. However, I knew that I had to forgive my parents because I knew that was a big chunk of where my problems stemmed. I immediately panicked and thought "how the fuck could I possibly do this when they have caused me such heartache?" I will tell you this, I decided. I know it sounds simple, but it truly was one of the biggest decisions in my life. I felt that I owed it to myself to at least try so I put on my best pair of big girl panties and threw myself into the unknown.

For the longest time I did not feel that the people who caused me pain deserve my forgiveness. I did not believe that I deserved my forgiveness. Does that sound familiar? Well, fucking stop it. Seriously. Right now. Because YOU do deserve it. Go ahead and roll your eyes at me, it's okay. I know that me telling you this doesn't make it true to you, it's a space you have to enter on your own. Even if you don't feel that whoever wronged you deserves it, remember this.....

Forgiving someone isn't excusing their behavior. Forgiving someone is giving yourself the peace you need to move past it.

95

Forgiving someone doesn't mean that you are suddenly best friends with them. You never have to confront them or pledge your forgiveness (unless you choose too). Forgiveness has nothing to do with them and what they did, it has everything to do with YOU. You hold onto it, hoping to .. what? Get back at them? Make them pay?

The only one living in misery was me. I was bitter, angry, and resentful. Nothing I could do TO anyone else would change that, the only thing any of us can ever change is ourselves. I decided to change how I felt. That's what forgiveness means to me.

Forgiving my parents took time. To be honest, it took A LOT of time. I was journaling, listening to podcasts, going to therapy, and I was using the forgiveness practice for months before I felt a shift.

The process helped me to move forward without feeling like I had an anchor around my neck. It has allowed me to be the parent I want to be not because I feel like I have to make up for the lack of parenting I received, but simply because I love my family and want to be the best mother that I can be. Forgiving myself for what I believed to be "bad decisions" has given me the freedom to see those decisions from a different perspective. Everything that I have done through forgiveness work has made me feel free from the burden of holding the anger in my body, my heart, my mind, my soul. It has allowed me to take my power back, to stop allowing the past to dictate my future.

I urge you to find time for forgiveness. Forgive yourself, forgive others. Lighten the load you carry around, see what freeing up the space that you devote to the anger, the resentment, and the pain can provide you.

Four Phrases To Change Your Life

I've used the Hawaiian practice of Ho'oponopono to allow me to offer forgiveness to myself and others. It's an incredibly powerful ritual that has a long history in the islands and was brought mainstream in the 70's. There has been so much research and reporting on it that all you have to do is Google it and you will be flooded with research and information. I have learned a great deal about the practice by following Dr. Hen Lew, an advocate and someone who is bringing new aspects and research to the practice. In its simplicity, it is a prayer of 4 phrases that you repeat over and over.

You can say it to others, you can say it to yourself, you can just say it in general. Spend as much time as you need practicing this ritual. It might not be a magic pill that you say 4 phrases one time and you are done. It's a process and that's okay. The anger and resentment didn't build up in a day so allow yourself time for the process to work.

I began a daily gratitude and forgiveness practice. I 100% went into this thinking that I would do this for a few days and I would magically let go of all the pain. The sun would shine down on me, I'd be surrounded by a cloud of iridescent glitter, and I'd hear angels singing. Shockingly, this was not the way. I spent weeks going through the forgiveness ritual and writing in a daily gratitude journal.

EVERY. SINGLE. DAY. I would wake up and go through my morning ritual. I had days where I felt so frustrated that nothing was changing, like what the fuck is the point in practicing this shit non-stop when I feel the same, I'm still hella pissed off, I feel like I was robbed of a childhood, and set up for failure as an adult. Why should I forgive ANY of that? Then I had days where I would go through gratitude, forgiveness, and meditation only to spend the rest of the day crying uncontrollably. Big ole ugly crying on and off throughout the entire day. When my husband would ask me what was wrong, I really couldn't even give him an answer. It was just my system working through all of the memories and emotions that my practice would bring up.

I was holding onto so much anger from my childhood. It left me feeling undeserving of love, of having success, of feeling at peace. I wanted to give up on the hope that anything was going to change. I had a "feeling" that I needed to keep going. You know that "feeling," that tingly feeling in the pit of your stomach, the hair on your neck stands up, your cheeks feel flushed, your inside is screaming at you to listen, your intuition. I listened and I kept going. I was not going to give up on something I knew, without a shadow of a doubt, that it was going to change my life. I kept going. Day after day, ugly cry after ugly cry, no change after no change. Until one day, as I was doing the practice, I did not feel the same anger when I said my parents' names. I continued the practice for another week and at the end of the week, I felt the shift. I was no longer consumed with the hurt that I felt they inflicted on me. I had come to the understanding that they are human beings who make mistakes and they provided what they had to offer, I can't expect more than that.

I meditate and journal every day. Now, life does happen and there are times when I do not get to complete my morning ritual. On days where I do not get that time to myself to start my day, I typically end up a little bitchy, just sayin'. I have discovered that my morning ritual time (even 10 minutes) is crucial to my wellbeing. It nurtures me mentally and spiritually, so I make every effort to allow myself that time each morning.

Journal It Out

- What does offering forgiveness mean to you?
- Are you holding onto grudges that are actually just holding YOU back?
- How do you think the ill-will you are harboring towards others affects them?
- Who do you need to forgive in order to start living the life you deserve?
- What is your Gremlin saying to you that you need to release?

- What does continuing to harbor all of this anger and angst provide for me?
- How is holding this pain, heartbreak, trauma, untrust, self-defeating thoughts, _____ in my body help me?
- What needs to happen for me to feel that I can entertain the thought of forgiveness for myself or for _____.

Forgiveness Work

Write your forgivness list.

I forgive myself for.......
I forgive my parents for........
I forgive my ex for........
I forgive my spouse for......
I forgive money for.......
Who/What else do you need to forgive? .

Ho'oponopono Prayer

I'm Sorry
Please Forgive Me
Thank you
I Love You

How To Use

After you create your list, repeat the prayer. Do this for each person/thing on your list until you feel yourself forgive. It may take several times of going through the steps. Be gentle with yourself and give yourself the necessary time you need. You may have been carrying these feelings around for years, you can't expect to release them. immediately. When you do feel ready to release, burn your list, let it go in the ocean, tear it up into tiny pieces, whatever works for you.

Eleven

Coming Full Circle

Lesson Learned

I have learned a shit ton of lessons over the course of my healing journey these last few years, but even beyond that, my 45 years of life, the moments, the experiences, the pains, and the joys, they have all shaped me into who I am today.

The people-pleasing served a purpose for a while, but I learned that I must also consider my own needs. I learned that perfection doesn't exist, it's nothing more than an unrealistic expectation we put on ourselves, which guarantees failure. I learned that when you are suffering from mental health concerns, when you are at the crumbling edge, you NEED to reach out for help. Ideally, before it ever even gets to that point. I have learned that our upbringing does not have to define our future. I have learned that we can take the pain and trauma we suffer and use it to propel us into the future we deserve and desire. I have learned that the limits we put on ourselves can be broken, the beliefs we hold may not even be our own and we can re-wire them. I have learned that it's okay to remove toxicity from your life, even when it's one of the hardest decisions you have to make. I have learned that I am worthy, that I matter.

I wish I would or could have asked for help sooner. I didn't really know I needed to and I honestly didn't know how to. That is why I wrote this book, for the version of me that needed it before I hit rock bottom and was googling ways to kill myself so my family would be okay. Writing this book has been just as much of a healing process for myself as I hope it becomes a tool of healing for you.

Worth It

Every path we take in life brings lessons. It's up to you how you react to those lessons, what you learn, what you repeat, what you grow through.

The alarm bells on my people-pleaser vault started going off when I tried to make changes and shifts in my life. DANGER, DANGER! You are going to piss people off, you are going to cause mass chaos, you don't know how to be anything EXCEPT a people-pleaser, who are you without that role? I had no idea how to be me without putting myself last. Creating a world where I was a priority was like starting all over. Like a baby learning to walk. I was heading into uncharted waters without a GPS and I was fucking scared. But I had a little voice inside my head (you know that mamma intuition stuff) that I typically ignore when it comes to my own well-being and FINALLY listened.

I learned enough from my past experiences to know that I was a good person, with a big heart, I was kind and thoughtful and I had a lot of love to give. I knew I deserved someone who could see that. I found that in my husband, but I also have come to find that within myself. Because self-love is not about identifying all the traits that make you imperfect, fixing them, and deciding that now you love yourself. It's about looking deeply within and finding gratitude for what you have and what you are in the moment.

I know that getting to a point where you can look at the pain or trauma you have experienced and then use it to help you heal can feel overwhelming. It might even sound like a big can of bullshit. I can share this with you now after years of doing the work, but when I was living through it, I would have never imagined it was something that would help me learn to love myself. The key to that sentence is that I have spent years putting in the work. I'm not saying it's easy. Shit, I still have trouble to this day. It is a conscious choice that you have to make. You have to decide if you deserve to be a priority in your own life (p.s. YOU DO).

Mindset Matters

One of the most important things I have learned over the last few years is that your mindset is key. That is why working with people like therapists on your trauma and with coaches on your mindset and going through your limiting beliefs can have such a massive impact on shifting your life. How you talk to yourself matters, how you talk to others matters, what you think and feel about every aspect of your day, matters.

While I say that what you say and think matters, understand that I am not a "positive vibes only" kinda gal. That is not at all what I'm saying. I do not believe for one fucking second that when you have a bad day/week/month that it will ruin everything, that you can't recover, that you have blocked all the "good" coming your way. I know that in the spiritual realm that is what a lot of people believe. That in order for you to manifest the life of your dreams, you have to be sunshine and rainbows all day, every day. I mean, let's be honest with ourselves, there is no fucking way that anyone can live their life that way. It's not realistic to think it's going to rain glitter down on you every day. Some days it's going to be a shit storm. I also believe it's important to work through the shitty, dark days. To sit with your feelings, to actually *feel them.* The trick is not to live in that space forever.

My Crown

I was in a coaching session with Ashley one day and we were discussing how I go about my day. I was talking about all of the routines and rituals that help me thrive and survive. From morning coffee with a book, to my daily journaling and meditation practice, and diffusing lavender at night. A ritual is something that you do with intention, mindfulness and purpose. That's the simplicity of it. Any act you perform can be turned into a ritual. That's the beauty of it. I showed her my post-it board that I call "Cactus Jack." It's a poster I stole from my daughter. Okay, not really stolen, she didn't want it and I was like, it's a cactus and the colors are awesome, I'm keeping it. I write notes, affirmations and reminders to myself on post-its and put them all over it. As part of my morning ritual, I read them. She was like "Holy shit you are like a queen of rituals!" A lightbulb flashed above my head and something clicked inside, YES, that feels right. And from that moment on, I became known as The Ritual Queen.

What does that mean? For me it meant acceptance. Not really from others, but from myself. The tiny, daily actions I take and tools I use for myself to care for myself. I have finally learned how to take care of myself, learned how to love myself, and learned how to flow with my emotions. My past, my depression, and my anxiety will always be part of me, there will always be wounds. Those are things I will continue to work on, but these are the things that have helped me become fully embodied and enjoying life. Listening to my passions, following my intuition, and discovering self-love and acceptance within. Turns out it's the small, little things after all. That's my secret sauce. That's what being The Ritual Queen means to me.

When you go through a gauntlet of experiences, including the pain and trauma, you have an opportunity to turn it into wisdom. Throughout my life, I have learned a variety of tools, routines, and rituals to help me grow and heal. I understand now when something is not working and can shift it. I also understand that what works for me may not work for someone else, we are all unique with our own needs. This is where support from someone who has been through it can help you. Sharing this wisdom is my calling. This is why I became a certified coach, to help others heal in the multitude of ways that are out there beyond the conventional. I focus on people's day to day, the habits that form our lives that can either hold us back or propel us forward. I prefer to call them rituals and with all I have been through, I decided to wear a fucking crown while doing it.

After reading my story and learning things about me that up until I wrote this, not many if any people even knew, I want to ask you: what does being a ritual queen mean to you? Share with me on social, send me a DM or an email, I would love to hear your response to this question.

With that said, my darlings, it's up to you now. It's your turn. Get help. You are just as worthy of the help you want to so willingly give away through people-pleasing. Allow yourself grace, understanding, and healing, find your voice, wear your fucking crown.

With love in my heart and light in my soul,
Theresa

P.S.
Always remember this:
You can't wear a crown if your head is down.

Journal It Out

- What does self-love mean to you?
- What does self-acceptance mean to you?
- Can you take one small action step today towards learning that acceptance? If yes, what will that action step be? If no, why not?
- What can you do for daily self-care that doesn't feel overwhelming?
- What does it mean to you to be a ritual queen?

How To Create A Ritual

A ritual is a routine that is done with purpose and intention.

• •

Start by listing all of your daily tasks. Include items that you "try to do" for yourself. You know, your self-care that always comes last.
Then decie what you can do with certaintiy and purpose. To make it even more intentional, create a sacred space to perform part of your ritual.

• •

Let me give you an example to make it clearer. My day goes like this.....I call it my "Start My Day Ritual"
I get my husband up for work, my daughter up for work or school if necessary, start my coffee, let my dogs out, Make my hubs breakfast, pack his lunch, send him on his way. Then I go tend to my chickens and ducks, water the flowers and garden (depending on time of day/heat, etc). Everyone else is taken care of now it's my time. I journal, meditate, pull cards, practice yoga, and read.
How is this a ritual?

Well, when I wake up, I set the INTENTION I want for the day, give it purpose. I do all of the things for my family and animals with love in my heart. When it's my time, I have a space in my office I've made "my sacred space" that I use or if it's nice outside that is where I go. I keep a basket in my "sacred space" that holds my journal, oracle cards, pens, books, etc. I just grab it and take it outside with me. Before I settle into my time, I reaffirm my intention with an affirmation and a few long, deep breathes.

Your Turn.....

Use this space to make a list of your daily activities, your routine and then decide how you can create the ritual with intention & purpose.

Resources – Essential Oil Blends

Seeing as how I am a Certified Aromatherapist and using essential oils was a big part of my recovery and pathway to self-care, I wanted to share with you some of my favorite blends. I use these in my diffusers at home on a daily basis.

Confident You
3d Grapefruit
2d Thyme ct thymol
1d Cardamom

Anxiety Sucks
5d Lavender
5d Lime
5d Mandarin (can substitute Sweet Orange)

Sigh Of Relief
5d Ravintsara
5d Tea Tree
5d Black Spruce

Clear The Air
5d Cedarwood

5d Orange

5d Frankincense

Calming

3d Lavender

3d Geranium

2d Chamomile (Roman or German)

2d Clary Sage

2d Ylang Ylang

Meditative Moments

3d Cedarwood

3d Lavender

2d Patchouli

Happy Vibes

4d Cedarwood

3d Lime

2d Lemon

Lift Me Up

2d Bergamot

2d Orange

2d Lemon

Resources – Forgiveness Work

Forgiveness Work

Write your forgivness list.

I forgive myself for.......
I forgive my parents for........
I forgive my ex for........
I forgive my spouse for......
I forgive money for.......
Who/What else do you need to forgive? .

Ho'oponopono Prayer

I'm Sorry
Please Forgive Me
Thank you
I Love You

How To Use

After you create your list, repeat the prayer. Do this for each person/thing on your list until you feel yourself forgive. It may take several times of going through the steps. Be gentle with yourself and give yourself the necessary time you need. You may have been carrying these feelings around for years, you can't expect to release them. immediately. When you do feel ready to release, burn your list, let it go in the ocean, tear it up into tiny pieces, whatever works for you.

Resources – Meet Gail

Meet G.A.I.L.

G This is getting in touch with the bitch voice in your head, your **Gremlin** as Ashley calls it.

A What are you **Assuming** about your life, relationships, finances, health, business, career, yourself?

I Your **Interpretation** of your life. Your judgement, opinions, and the filter you view through.

L What are your **Limiting** Beliefs?

- Start with **G**, name your Gremlin, what is your gremlin saying to you, about you?
- Next is **A**, write out your assumptions about your life - ALL of them, in ALL areas.
- Move onto **I**, how are you interpreting your life, is it hard, will you always struggle, will you always be addicted, will you always be alone, how are you judging yourself?
- Lastly we have **L**, this is where you get the chance to write out all of the beliefs you have that are limiting your movement, your progress, your success.

Now that you have identities all of these assumptions, judgements, and beliefs, you can begin to work through them, reframe them, shift them, heal them.

Resources – Affirmations

Self-Love Affirmations

- I am full of joy and gratitude.
- I love myself just the way I am.
- I am abundant.
- I am beautiful.
- I am enough, I have enough, I do enough.
- I am full of love and radiate it outward.
- My life is meaningful.
- I love my body and all it has done for me and will do for me.
- I learn and grow everyday
- I am powerful, I am strong, I am worthy.
- I deserve all the good that is coming my way.
- I acknowledge my own self-worth.
- I am worthy of love and connection
- My perfect partner loves me exactly as I am
- I deserve to have everything I want out of this life.

Angel Numbers Guidebook

A GUIDE TO

understanding

ANGEL NUMBERS

The Universe is always around us communicating. It's our job to be aware and open.

If you have been seeing Angel Numbers all around and want to know more about what they mean, this is for you.

What does it mean if I see "0"s

0 symbolizes oneness and connectedness.
A fresh start & new beginnings.
When you are seeing 0's or a sequence of
0's, it's a reminder that you are the creator
of your own destiny.

What does it mean if I see "1"s

1 symbolizes alignment, independence and
new creation.
It's a sign you are on the right path.
It's also a sign you are in the presence of
angels.
A reminder to ensure you are focusing on
what you want.

What does it mean if I see "2's

2 symbolizes responsibility and a sign to keep moving forward. Everything is working out as it should.
Stay positive and stay the course.

What does it mean if I see "3's

3 symbolizes the union of mind, body & spirit.
It's a reminder to stop doubting yourself and to take action.
The angels want you to know it's okay to ask for help, you are being guided.

What does it mean if I see "4"s

4 symbolizes stability and order.
It's a reminder to continue doing the inner work.
It's also to let you know you are surrounded by your angels and being guided.

What does it mean if I see "5"s

5 symbolizes change and grace.
It's a sign to prepare for big changes and transitions in your life that are for your highest good.

What does it mean if I see "6"s

6 symbolizes material goods and matters.
It's a sign to refocus your attention back to
spirituality and faith.
Remember to express gratitude.
A reminder to listen to your intuition and
find a balance.

What does it mean if I see "7"s

7 symbolizes luck and encouragement. It's
a reminder that you are fully supported
and on the right track.
It can symbolize being in flow of
manifesting your dreams.

What does it mean if I see "8's

8 symbolizes infinity. All that is good.
Abundance. Abundance. Abundance.
In all areas of your life.
A divine sign that your prayers are heard
and being answered.

What does it mean if I see "9's

9 symbolizes that you may need to be of
service.
It could be a sign of needing to complete
a project you have started but yet to
finish.
It can also be a sign of needing to connect
to your souls mission.

REVIVE AND THRIVE Ritual

5 Simple Steps

Why would someone have a daily ritual practice?
I've suffered from anxiety and depression for many years. I also lost my identity after years of people pleasing. I wrapped up who I was in being a mom, I had no sense of self outside of that. I spent a lot of time allowing those things to control my life.

Until I decided that I was deserving of spending time focusing on myself. I was worthy of discovering who I was and honoring myself.

This took time and that time became sacred to me. I started creating rituals to help me get back in touch with who I am, with my purpose, with my soul.

I created the Revive & Thrive Ritual to share with you because I believe 1,000% in the power of rituals and how they can bring you back to yourself. What if there was a way that you could not only survive your day but thrive through it? You would give it a try right? What's the worse thing that can happen from allowing yourself 15 - 30 minutes a day all to yourself?

This process can help you to start your day from a place of calmness, being thankful and energized. I am going to break down for you, how to incorporate these 5 steps into your day as well as helping you understand

124

why it's important and the difference it can make in your life.

So what exactly is Revive & Thrive?

The five elements of the ritual are meditation, journaling, gratitude, movement and hydration. All 5 work together to provide you a foundation of success on which to build your day.

Step 1, Journaling

Let's start with a few ideas of why you should give it a try, a few ways it has helped me.

-Heal
-Vent
-Goals & Dreams
-Find Your Inspiration
-East Stress & Anxiety

Journaling doesn't need to be fancy, you don't need a special expensive book and you do not need to be articulate or concern yourself with proper punctuation. It's all about you getting what you need out and down on paper. There is something powerful about putting words and thoughts to paper. It's a way for you to get out your feelings to allow you to heal from pain or trauma or hurt caused by others. It's a way to vent when you need to get something off your chest but don't want any confrontation. When you want to explore your dreams, when you want to write down your goals to help turn it more into a plan, journaling is the perfect medium to do this activity. You can randomly write daily when you don't know what to say, this is a perfect way to help find your inspiration. This idea comes from the book "The Artists Way" by Julie Cameron. Getting all your thoughts and feelings out and onto paper is a great method of reducing your stress and anxiety.

Doing some additional research on how journaling can benefit you provided some that surprised me. A few of those were sharpening memory, improved immune function, solve problems efficiently, and resolve disagreements. A few others were reducing stress, boosting your mood, cope with depression, clarify your thoughts
and feelings and getting to know yourself better. As you can see, the benefits of journaling go far beyond just putting thoughts to paper. When this is something you do constantly it has
amazing emotional, physical, spiritual and possibly physical benefits. Something that you can do at zero cost that can improve your life? Yes please.

Step 2, Meditation

What even is meditation? It is a practice where you use techniques to train your attention, awareness and achieve mental clarity and an emotionally calm and stable state. Sounds heavenly right? It's been reported that meditation can be dated by to as early as 5,000 BCE with written evidence of any form first seen in Vedas
around 1500 BCE. There have been numerous studies on its effectiveness with anxiety, pain, depression, PTSD, sleep, heart disease and so much more. It is believed it can positively impact mental and physical health.
I love this quote but I can't tell you who said it. "The quality of your mind determines the quality of your life."

Here are a few ways that a daily meditation practice can help you as it's helped me.
-Focus
-Clarity
-Serenity
-Breathe Deep, Breath-work
-Observe Feelings, Inward Connection

Of course these are only a few of the benefits of meditation that helped me personally. A few more that I found listed on The Mayo Clinic are as follows: gaining a new perspective, manage stress, increase self-awareness, help focus on the present, reduce negative emotions, increase creativity, patience & tolerance. I continued my research and on Healthline.com I found additional research had been done that includes even more benefits. Those benefits include decreased blood pressure, pain control, improvement of sleep, help in fighting addiction, generate kindness, reduce age related memory loss, lengthen your attention span, promote emotional health. The great thing about meditation is you can do it anywhere and for any amount of time. There is no right or wrong way to do it. On my busiest days I will add it in during a shower. I close my eyes while the water is running over my head, take a few deep breathes, then imagine whatever is blocking me, any negativity taking over, being washed away by the pure clear water. Then I picture those negative feelings or blocks as a color and watch them go down the drain. Then I visualize the pure, clear water restoring me as it washes over my body.
You can find 3-5 minutes in your day to get quiet, breathe deep and meditate.

Step 3, Gratitude

Gratitude turns what we have into enough. -Melody Beattle

There have been scientifically proven benefits to maintaining a gratitude practice. Some of those benefits include opening the door to more relationships. Improve physical and psychological health. Help enhance empathy and reduce aggression. It's been shown to help you sleep better, improve your self-esteem and increase your mental strength. There have been numerous studies that show grateful people have higher levels of happiness and lower levels of stress or depression. Those sound like some amazing benefits for an easy practice that doesn't take much time. The way I started practicing gratitude was just by

saying out-loud
what I was grateful for every morning. I started to do this before my feet
even hit the floor. Then I'd follow up it up with more positive and thankful
thoughts as I finished my morning hygiene
routine. You can advance your practice by starting a gratitude journal. The
point is to find what
works for you.

Step 4, Movement

Now, this may not be a favorite of everyones. I know that this one has been
a struggle for myself. I'm pretty hot or cold when it comes to "exercise" so
instead I started looking at it as movement. My body is happy when I spend
a few minutes moving it to start my day. This can be as simple as 5 minutes
stretching. A yoga routine. A walk with your dog or by yourself. An actual
workout. Whatever level of physical activity you prefer and if it's something
that you resist, start small with stretching or a light yoga routine. Let's go
over some of the benefits I found when doing my research. Let's start with
my personal favorite, Yoga. It improves strength, balance and flexibility. It
can help manage stress, increase energy and promote better sleep.

A general research of exercise benefits returned the following: improve
memory, protect against chronic disease, control weight, boost energy,
improve your mood, spark your sex life and promote better sleep.

While exercise may seem daunting and overwhelming to someone who
doesn't have a usual fitness ritual, it can be started in small steps. Like I
mentioned above, start with stretching or a 10 minute yoga routine or a
short walk around the neighborhood. Work your way up to exercise
equipment or longer, more intense routines. YouTube is a great place to find
video's to get you started for any of the above.

Step 5, Lemon Water

Water in general is a necessity of life. Keeping yourself hydrated promotes cardiovascular health, supple skin, helps muscles and joins work better, keeps your body cool, and cleanses your body both inside & out. So drinking water throughout the day is very key to your overall health and wellbeing. But the benefits of beginning your day with lemon water (yes before coffee) have been astonishing to me.

Here are a few that I have experienced.

*Helps with digestion

*Fresher breathe

*Energy boost

*Increased hydration throughout day

*Lower blood pressure

The additional research I found showed that drinking lemon water can supply you with vitamin C, give you a potassium boost, help prevent kidney stones, prevent oxidation, it's weight-loss friendly, help with inflammation and can improve your skin quality. How should you make it? How much should you drink? Truth is it doesn't matter, anyway you do it will be a boost!

Start with 1/2 lemon squeezed into a glass of water and adjust to your tastes.

That's it. That is the 5 step ritual that you can incorporate into your day in as little as 15-30 minutes to make massive impact in your life.

If you would like a printable PDF of the ritual along with some journaling prompts, go to

https://www.subscribepage.com/e7t2v5

Acknowledgements

Earl aka the love of my life, my BFF. Thank you for knocking me up and creating this perfectly imperfect life with me. Without you there is no me.

My children, Earl & Darian aka my gift to the world. Thank you for allowing me to be your mother. For teaching me what true unconditional love is all about. For just being you. I love you both with all of my being, you are my world.

Aunt Sissy & Uncle Bob aka Mom & Dad. Thank you isn't quite enough. I would not be the person I am today without your love, support, and influence in my life.

Bonnie & Earl aka the most amazing in-laws a girl could ask for. Thank you for accepting me into your family with open arms and loving me as if I was one of your own children. Thank you for gifting me with your son, he's a pretty bomb-ass guy.

The entire Tirk Clan aka my family. Thank you for welcoming me into the family and treating me like I was one of you, for loving me and supporting me for the last 20+ years. I love each and every one of you.

Wendy Cubero aka my bomb ass therapist. I mean, what can I say. Without your guidance & support, I would not have had the strength and courage to write this book.

Ashley Gordon aka Goddess of Big Coach Energy & my mentor. The first person who had such faith in me and my potential to follow my path of purpose and never gave up me when I was so fucking stubborn and trying to resist. Thank you for being the badass coach that you are and pulling out all that needed to be released to allow me to get here. Love you girl.

My QCA Family aka the support system that allowed me to step into being ME. I am honored to be friends with this powerhouse group of such dynamic women, I love you all.

Jess Nichol aka my book writing savior, editor & life-line. I am so thankful that QCA brought us together because this book would not be in the hands of others without you! You never gave up on me when I got super fucking cranky and irritable with the process. Thank you for believing in me and in this book to constantly push me out of my comfort zone.

Vanessa Love aka Goddess of Energy & my Reiki Master. You opened my eyes to what is possible. You keep me open to all the wondrous possibilities while being grounded in my purpose. We are so connected and I am forever grateful that the Universe brought us together.

Amber Rose aka the best fucking agent EVER. I will be forever grateful that you slid into my DM's. Thank you for having such faith in this book before you ever even read the entire thing. Thank you for believing in me and my message and being the driving force behind allowing it to get out into the world. You are such an influence to me and I am honored to be your client and your friend. This is just the beginning of our journey together and I can't wait for what's to come. Thank you for everything!

About the Author

Theresa Tirk is an Author, Public Speaker, Certified Aromatherapist, Spiritual Life Coach dedicated to helping women everywhere awaken to their own validation and strength so they can step out of overwhelm and back into joy. She began coaching after her own spiritual journey of self-discovery through a battle with depression and anxiety. She believes in the power of mindset shifts and creating daily rituals that have massive impact on your life. She is the CEO of The Ritual Queen LLC and host of The Ritual Queen Podcast. When she is not working, her favorite place to be is with her husband and kids. Preferably sitting on a beach somewhere.

You can connect with me on:

🌐 https://www.theritualqueen.com

Also by The Ritual Queen

Be Uncensored: The Coloring Book

Get Uncensored: The Journal

Printed in Great Britain
by Amazon